Mosby's War
REMINISCENCES

Some of Mosby's Men

Mosby's War
REMINISCENCES
Stuart's Cavalry
CAMPAIGNS

By John S. Mosby

JOHN CULLER & SONS
CAMDEN, SOUTH CAROLINA

1996

DESIGNED BY ANN C. JENNINGS

ISBN 1-887269-09-6

LIBRARY OF CONGRESS CATALOG
CARD NUMBER: 96-83518

JOHN CULLER & SONS
P.O. BOX 1227
CAMDEN, SOUTH CAROLINA 29020
(803) 432-2001

CONTENTS.

CHAPTER VIII.

CHAPTER IX.

CHAPTER X.

CHAPTER XI.

CHAPTER XII.

CHAPTER XIII.

CHAPTER XIV.

MOSBY'S WAR REMINISCENCES.

CHAPTER I.

"Rebellion!
How many a spirit born to bless,
  Hath sunk beneath that withering name,
Whom but a day's — an hour's — success
  Had wafted to eternal fame." — *Tom Moore.*

IN April, 1861, I was attending court at Abingdon, Va., when I met a person who had just stepped out of the telegraph office, who informed me that tremendous tidings were passing over the wires. Going in, I inquired of the operator what it was, who told me that Lincoln had issued a proclamation calling out troops. Fort Sumter had fallen two days before. The public mind was already strained to a high pitch of excitement, and it required only a spark to produce an explosion. The indignation aroused by the President's proclamation spread like fire on a prairie, and the laws became silent in the midst of arms. People of every age, sex, and condition were borne away on the tide of excited feeling that swept over the land.

The home of Gov. John B. Floyd, who had resigned
as secretary of war under Buchanan, was at Abingdon. I went to his house and told him the news.
He immediately issued a call to arms, which resounded like the roll of Ziska's drum among the
mountains of southwestern Virginia. Many of the
most influential families in that region were descend-
ants of the men who had fought under Morgan and
Campbell at Eutaw Springs and King's Mountain.
Their military spirit was inflamed by stirring appeals
to the memories of the deeds their sires had done.
Women, too, came forward to inspire men with a
spirit of heroic self-sacrifice, and a devotion that
rivalled the maidens of Carthage and Saragossa.

All the pride and affection that Virginians had
felt in the traditions of the government which their
ancestors had made, and the great inheritance which
they had bequeathed, were lost in the overpowering
sentiment of sympathy with the people who were
threatened with invasion. It is a mistake to suppose
that the Virginia people went to war in obedience
to any decree of their State, commanding them to
go. On the contrary, the people were in a state of
armed revolution before the State had acted in its
corporate capacity. I went along with the flood like
everybody else. A few individuals here and there
attempted to breast the storm of passion, and ap-

peared like Virgil's ship-wrecked mariners, "Rari nantes in surgite vasto." Their fate did not encourage others to follow their example, and all that they did was to serve "like ocean wrecks to illuminate the storm." In anticipation of these events, a cavalry company had for some months been in process of organization, which I had joined as a private. This company — known as the Washington Mounted Rifles — was immediately called together by its commanding officer, Capt. William E. Jones. Capt. Jones was a graduate of West Point, and had resigned some years before from the United States army. He was a stern disciplinarian, and devoted to duty. Under a rugged manner and impracticable temper he had a heart that beat with warm impulses. To his inferiors in rank he was just and kind, but too much inclined to cross the wishes and criticise the orders of his superiors. He had been a classmate of Stonewall Jackson at the military academy, and related to me many anecdotes of Jackson's piety, as well as his eccentricities. He was a hard swearer; and a few days after the battle of Bull Run he told me that he was at Jackson's headquarters, and Jackson got very much provoked at something a soldier had done, when Jones said, "Jackson, let me cuss him for you." He fell in battle with Gen. Hunter, in the valley of Virginia, in June, 1864. We went into barracks at Abingdon, and began drilling.

No service I ever had to perform during the war went as much against the grain as standing guard the first night I was in camp. I had no friends in the cavalry company, so I applied to Gov. Litchen for a transfer to an infantry company that had been raised in that part of the county where I resided. But on the very day I made the application, a telegraphic order came for us to start for Richmond immediately, and I never heard anything more of it. My company marched on horseback all the way to Richmond — about five hundred miles — while the infantry company went by rail. But how small is the control that mortals have over their own destinies. The company to which I unsuccessfully applied to be transferred became a part of the immortal division of Stonewall Jackson, in which I would have had only a slight chance of asserting my individuality, which would have been merged in the mass. I remember distinctly, now, how with a heart almost bursting with grief, in the midst of a rain, I bade my friends in the infantry company farewell just as they were about getting on the train. I had no dream then that I would ever be anything more than a private soldier. On the same day in rain and mud we started on the march to Richmond. A few days before a flag had been presented to our company by a young lady, with an address in which she reminded us that "the coward dies a thousand deaths — the brave man dies but one." I am sure there was not a man among us who did not feel the ambition of the youth in Longfellow's poem, bearing

> Onward amid the ice and snow of Alpine heights
> His banner with its strange device.

The march to Richmond under a soldier who had bivouacked on the plains was a course of beneficial discipline. The grief of parting from home and friends soon wore away, and we all were as gay as if we were going to a wedding or a picnic. Gloom was succeeded by mirth and songs of gladness, and if Abraham Lincoln could have been sung out of the South as James II. was out of England, our company would have done it and saved the country all the fighting. The favorite songs were generally those of sentiment and sadness, intermingled with an occasional comic melody. I remember this refrain of one that often resounded from the head to the rear of the column as we passed some farmer's house:

> He who has good buttermilk a plenty, and gives the soldiers none,
> He shan't have any of our buttermilk when his buttermilk is gone.

The buttermilk, as well as everything else that the farmer had that was good, was generally given

to the soldiers. The country was brimful of patriotism.

The gayety with which men marched into the face
of death is not so remarkable as the fortitude and
cheerfulness of the wives and mothers who stayed
at home and waited for the news of the battles.
In nearly every home of the South could be found
an example of that Spartan mother who sent her
son to the wars with her last injunction to return
with his shield or return upon it. This courage,
exhibited in the beginning, survived to the last,
through all the long agony and bloody sweat of the
struggle. On reaching Richmond, after a few days'
rest, we were ordered to the Shenandoah valley.
A day or so before we started, Capt. Jones made
a requisition on the quartermaster's department for
clothing for his company. We were furnished with
suits of a very rough quality of goods manufactured
in the Virginia penitentiary. It almost produced a
mutiny in the camp. The men piled the clothes
up in front of the captain's tent. Only two refused
to wear them — Private Fountain Beattie and myself. I do not think any clothes I ever wore did
me more service than these. When I became a
commander I made Beattie a lieutenant. I think we
were both as contented on the picket line, dressed
in our penitentiary suits, as we ever were in the

gay uniforms we afterwards wore. Our march from Richmond to the Shenandoah valley was an ovation — our people had had no experiences of the misery and desolation that follow in the track of war; they were full of its romance, and expected us to win battles that would rival the glories of Wagram and Marengo. They never counted the cost of victory.

Our company was incorporated into the 1st regiment of Virginia cavalry, commanded by Col. J. E. B. Stuart. It was stationed at a village called Bunker Hill, on the turnpike leading from Winchester to Martinsburg, and was observing the Union army under Patterson, which was then stationed at the latter place, on the Baltimore & Ohio Railroad. Gen. Joseph E. Johnston then had his headquarters at Winchester. I first saw Stuart at Bunker Hill. He had then lately resigned from the United States army to link his fortunes with the Southern Confederacy. He was just twenty-eight years of age — one year older than myself — strongly built, with blue eyes, ruddy complexion, and a reddish beard. He wore a blouse and foraging cap with a linen cover, called a havelock, as a protection against the sun. His personal appearance indicated the distinguishing traits of his character — dash, great strength of will, and indomitable energy. Stuart soon showed that he possessed all the qualities of a great leader of cavalry — a sound judgment, a quick intelligence to penetrate the designs of an enemy, mingled with the brilliant courage of Rupert.

There was then such a wide chasm between me and him that I was only permitted to view him at a distance, and had no thought of ever rising to intimacy with him.   He took us the next day on a scout down toward Martinsburg and gave us our first lesson in war and sight of the enemy.   We saw the hills around the town covered with the white tents of the Union army, and caught two soldiers who had ventured too far outside the picket lines.   Since then I have witnessed the capture of thousands, but have never felt the same joy as I did over these first two prisoners.

A few days after this, Patterson started out on a promenade toward Winchester, and then turned squarely off, and went back toward Charlestown. Patterson made a good deal of noise with the shells that he threw at us, but nobody was hurt.   Stuart kept close on his flanks, both to watch his movements and to screen Johnston's, who had just begun to move to join Beauregard at Manassas.   Fitz John Porter and George H. Thomas, who afterward became distinguished generals, were on his staff. Patterson has been greatly censured for not pressing Johnston, and detaining him in the Shenandoah valley, instead of making the retrograde movement to Charlestown that permitted his escape. He alleges that he acted under the advice of his staff officers. Patterson was a conspicuous figure as well as failure in the first scene of the first act of the drama of war; after that he disappeared forever. His campaign in the Shenandoah valley was a mere prologue to the great tragedy that was afterward acted there. Stuart left him in a position where he could neither be of advantage to the cause he upheld nor injury to that he opposed, and crossed the Blue Ridge to take part in the battle of Bull Run, on the 21st of July.

CHAPTER II.

"O! shadow of glory — dim image of war —
The chase hath no story — her hero no star."
— *Byron, Deformed Transformed.*

AFTER the first battle of Bull Run, Stuart's cavalry was engaged in performing outpost duty on our front, which extended from the falls above Washington to Occoquan, on the lower Potomac. There were no opportunities for adventurous enterprise. McClellan's army was almost in a state of siege in Washington, and his cavalry but rarely showed themselves outside his infantry picket line. We had to go on picket duty three times a week and remain twenty-four hours. The work was pretty hard; but still, soldiers liked it better than the irksome life of the camp. I have often sat alone on my horse from midnight to daybreak, keeping watch over the sleeping army. During this period of inaction, the stereotyped message sent every night from Washington to the northern press was, "All quiet along the Potomac."

While I was a private in Stuart's cavalry, I never missed but one tour of outpost duty, and then I was confined in the hospital from an injury. With one other, I was stationed at the post on the road leading from Fall's Church to Lewinsville, in Fairfax. At night we relieved each other alternately, one sleeping while the other watched. About dusk, Capt. Jones had ridden to the post and instructed us that we had no troops outside our lines on that road, and that we must fire, without halting, on any body of men approaching from that direction, as they would be the enemy. The night was dark, and it had come my turn to sleep. I was lying on the ground, with the soft side of a stone for a pillow, when I was suddenly aroused by my companion, who called to me to mount, that the Yankees were coming. In an almost unconscious state I leaped into my saddle, and at the same instant threw forward my carbine, and both of us fired on a body of cavalry not fifty yards distant. Fortunately, we fired so low our bullets struck the ground just in front of them. The flash from my carbine in my horse's face frightened him terribly. He wheeled, and that is the last I remember about that night. The next thing I recollect is that some time during the next day I became conscious, and found myself lying on a bed at the house of the keeper of the toll-gate. Capt. Jones and several of the men of my company were standing by me. It appears that the night before Stuart had sent a company of cavalry to Lewinsville for some purpose. This company had gone out by one road and returned on the one where I had been posted. My horse had run away and fallen over a cow that was lying down, and rolled over me. The company of cavalry coming along the same way, their horses in front started and snorted at something lying in the road. They halted, some of them dismounted to see what it was, and discovered me there in an insensible state. They picked me up and carried me into the village, apparently dying. I was bruised from head to foot, and felt like every bone in my body had been broken. I had to be carried to Fairbay Court House in an ambulance. There is a tradition that when Capt. Jones looked on me that night he swore harder than the army in Flanders. The feelings he expressed for the officer in fault were not so benevolent as my Uncle Toby's for the fly.

While the cavalry did not have an opportunity to do much fighting during the first year of the war, they learned to perform the duties and endure the privations of a soldier's life. My experience in this school was of great advantage to me in the after years when I became a commander. There was a thirst for adventure among the men in the cavalry, and a positive pleasure to get an occasional

shot "from a rifleman hid in a thicket." There
were often false alarms, and sometimes real ones,
from scouting parties of infantry who would come
up at night to surprise our pickets. A vivid imagination united with a nervous temperament can see
in the dark the shapes of many things that have no
real existence. A rabbit making its nocturnal rounds,
a cow grazing, a hog rooting for acorns, an owl
hooting, or the screech of a night hawk could often
arouse and sometimes stampede an outpost or draw
the fire of a whole line of pickets. At the first shot,
the reserve would mount; and soon the videttes
would come running in at full speed. There was
an old gray horse roaming about the fields at Fairfax
Court House during the first winter of the war that
must have been fired at a hundred times at night
by our videttes, and yet was never touched. I have
never heard whether Congress has voted him a pen-
sion. The last time that I was ever on picket was
in February, 1862. The snow was deep and hard
frozen. My post was on the outskirts of Fairfax
Court House, at the junction of the Washington
road and turnpike. I wore a woollen hood to keep
my ears from freezing, and a blanket thrown around
me as a protection against the cold wind. The
night was clear, and all that's best of dark and
bright. I sat on my horse under the shadow of

a tree, both as a protection from the piercing blast
and as a screen from the sight of an enemy. I had
gone on duty at midnight, to remain until daybreak.
The deep silence was occasionally broken by the cry
of "Halt!" from some distant sentinel, as he chal-
lenged the patrol or relief. The swaying branches
of the trees in the moonlight cast all sorts of fan-
tastic forms on the crystal snow. In this deep soli-
tude, I was watching for danger and communing
with the spirit of the past. At this very spot, a few
nights before, the vidette had been fired on by a
scouting party of infantry that had come up from
McClellan's camps below. But the old gray horse
had several times got up a panic there which raised
a laugh on the soldiers.

Now I confess that I was about as much afraid of
ridicule as of being shot, and so, unless I got killed
or captured, I resolved to spend the night there.
Horatius Cocles was not more determined to hold his
position on the bridge of the Tiber, than I was to
stay at my post, but perhaps his motives were less
mixed than mine. I had been long pondering and
remembering, and in my reverie had visited the fields
that I had traversed "in life's morning march when
my bosom was young." I was suddenly aroused by
the crash of footsteps breaking the crust of the hard
snow. The sound appeared to proceed from some-

thing approaching me with the measured tread of a
file of soldiers. It was screened from my view by
some houses near the roadside. I was sure that it
was an enemy creeping up to get a shot at me, for I
thought that even the old horse would not have ventured out on such a night, unless under orders. My
heart began to sicken within me pretty much like
Hector's did when he had to face the wrath of
Achilles. My horse, shivering with cold, with the
instinct of danger, pricked up his ears and listened
as eagerly as I did to the footsteps as they got near.
I drew my pistol, cocked it, and took aim at the corner around which this object must come. I wanted
to get the advantage of the first shot. Just then the
hero of a hundred panics appeared — the old gray
horse! I returned my pistol to my belt and relapsed
into reverie. I was happy: my credit as a soldier
had been saved.

A couple of days after this my company returned
there, as usual, on picket. On this same morning
Stuart came, making an inspection of the outposts.
It happened that there were two young ladies living
at Fairfax Court House, acquaintances of his, who
did not like to stay in such an exposed situation, and
so Stuart had arranged to send them to the house of
a friend near Fryingpan, which was further within our
lines. At that time the possibility of our army ever

retiring to Richmond had not been conceived by the
rank and file. Stuart had then become a brigadier-
general, and Capt. Jones had been promoted to be
colonel of the 1st Virginia cavalry. Although I
served under Stuart almost from the beginning of
the war, I had no personal acquaintance with him
before then. He asked Capt. Blackford to detail
a man to go along as an escort for the two ladies.
I had often been invited to the house of one of them
by her father, so I was selected on that account to
go with them. I left my horse with my friend
Beattie to lead back to camp, and took a seat in
the carriage with the ladies. This was on the 12th
of February, 1862. It began snowing just as we
started, and it was late in the afternoon before we
got to Fryingpan. I then went in the carriage to
Stuart's headquarters a few miles off, at Centreville.
It was dark when I got there. I reported to him the
result of my mission to Fryingpan, and asked for a
pass to go back to the camp of my regiment, which
was about four miles off on Bull Run. Stuart told
me that the weather was too bad for me to walk to
camp that night, but to stay where I was until next
morning. He and Generals Joseph E. Johnston and
G. W. Smith occupied the Grigsby house and messed
together. I sat down by a big wood fire in an open
fireplace in the front room, where he and the other

two generals were also sitting. I never spoke a word, and would have been far happier trudging through the snow back to camp, or even as a vidette on a picket post. I felt just as much out of place and uneasy as a mortal would who had been lifted to a seat by the side of the gods on Olympus. Presently supper was announced. The generals all walked into the adjoining room, and Stuart told me to come in. After they had sat down at the table, Stuart observed that I was not there and sent for me. I was still sitting by the fire. I obeyed his summons like a good soldier, and took my place among the *dii majores*. I was pretty hungry, but did not enjoy my supper. I would have preferred fasting or eating with the couriers. I know I never spoke a word to any one — I don't think I raised my eyes from off my plate while I was at the table.

Now, while I felt so much oppressed by the presence of men of such high rank, there was nothing in their deportment that produced it. It was the same way the next morning. Stuart had to send after me to come in to breakfast. I went pretty much in the same dutiful spirit that Gibbon says that he broke his marriage engagement: "I sighed as a lover and obeyed as a son." But now my courage rose; I actually got into conversation with Joe Johnston, whom I would have regarded it as a great privilege the day before to view through a long-range telescope. The generals talked of Judah P. Benjamin's (who was then Secretary of War) breach of courtesy to Stonewall Jackson that had caused Jackson to send in his resignation. They were all on Jackson's side. There was nothing going on about Centreville to indicate the evacuation that took place three weeks after that. Stuart let me have a horse to ride back to camp. As soon as I got there, Col. Jones sent for me to come to his tent. I went, and he offered me the place of adjutant of the regiment. I had had no more expectation of such a thing than of being translated on Elijah's chariot to the skies. Of course, I accepted it. I was never half as much frightened in any fight I was in as I was on the first dress parade I conducted. But I was not permitted to hold the position long. About two months after that, when we had marched to meet McClellan at Yorktown, my regiment reorganized under the new act of the Confederate Congress. Fitz Lee was elected colonel in place of Jones. This was the result of an attempt to mix democracy with military discipline. Fitz Lee did not reappoint me as adjutant, and so I lost my first commission on the spot where Cornwallis lost his sword. This was at the time an unrecognized favor. If I had been retained as adjutant, I would probably have never been anything else. So at the close of the first year of the war I was, in point of rank, just where I had begun. Well, it did not break my heart. When the army was retiring from Centreville, Stuart's cavalry was the rear guard, and I had attracted his favorable notice by several expeditions I had led to the rear of the enemy. So Stuart told me to come to his headquarters and act as a scout for him. A scout is not a spy who goes in disguise, but a soldier in arms and uniform, who goes among as enemy's lines to get information about them. Among the survivors of the Army of the Potomac there are many legends afloat, and religiously believed to be true, of a mysterious person — a sort of Flying Dutchman or Wandering Jew — prowling among their camps in the daytime in the garb of a beggar or with a pilgrim's staff, and leading cavalry raids upon them at night. In popular imagination, I have been identified with that mythical character.

On the day after Mr. Lincoln's assassination, Secretary Stanton telegraphed to Gen. Hancock, then in command at Winchester, Va., that I had been seen at the theatre in Washington on that fatal night. Fortunately, I could prove an alibi by Hancock himself, as I was at that very time negotiating a truce with him. I recently heard an officer of the United States army tell a story of his being with the guard for a wagon train, and my passing him

with my command on the pike, all of us dressed as
Federal soldiers, and cutting the train out from
behind him. I laughed at it, like everybody who
heard it, and did not try to unsettle his faith. To
have corrected it would have been as cruel as to
dispel the illusion of childhood that the story of
" Little Red Riding Hood " is literally true, or to
doubt the real presence of Santa Claus. It was all
pure fiction about our being dressed in blue uniforms, or riding with him. I did capture the wagon
train at the time and place mentioned, Oct. 26, 1863,
at the Chestnut Fork, near Warrenton, Va., but we
never even saw the guard. They had got sleepy,
and gone on to camp, and left me to take care of
their wagons — which I did. The quartermaster in
charge of them, Capt. Stone, who was made prisoner, called to pay his respects to me a few days
ago. I can now very well understand how the
legendary heroes of Greece were created. I always
wore the Confederate uniform, with the insignia of
my rank. So did my men. So any success I may
have had, either as an individual scout or partisan
commander, cannot be accounted for on the theory
that it was accomplished through disguise. The
hundreds of prisoners I took are witnesses to the
contrary.

FAUQUIER COUNTY, VA., Feb. 4, 1863.

GENERAL : — I arrived in this neighborhood about one week ago. Since then I have been, despite the bad weather, quite actively engaged with the enemy. The result up to this time has been the capture of twenty-eight Yankee cavalry together with all their horses, arms, etc. The evidence of parole I forward with this. I have also paroled a number of deserters. Col. Sir Percy Wyndham, with over two hundred cavalry, came up to Middleburg last week to punish me, as he said, for my raids on his picket line. I had a slight skirmish with him, in which my loss was three men, captured by the falling of their horses ; the enemy's loss, one man and three horses captured. He set a very nice trap a few days ago to catch me in. I went into it, but, contrary to the Colonel's expectations, brought the trap off with me, killing one, capturing twelve ; the balance running. The extent of the annoyance I have been to the Yankees may be judged of by the fact that, baffled in their attempts to capture me, they threaten to retaliate on citizens for my acts.

I forward to you some correspondence I have had on the subject. The most of the infantry has left Fairfax and gone towards Fredericksburg. In Fairfax there are five or six regiments of cavalry ; there are about three hundred at Dranesville. They are so isolated from the rest of the command, that nothing would be easier than their capture. I have harassed them so much that they do not keep their pickets over half a mile from camp. There is no artillery there. I start on another trip day after to-morrow.

I am, most respectfully, yours, etc.,

JOHN S. MOSBY.

MAJ.-GEN. J. E. B. STUART.

HEADQUARTERS CAVALRY DIVISION, Feb. 8, 1863.

Respectfully forwarded as additional proof of the prowess, daring, and efficiency of Mosby (without commission) and his band of a dozen chosen spirits.

J. E. B. STUART,
Major-General Commanding.

HEADQUARTERS, Feb. 11, 1863.

Respectfully forwarded to the Adjutant and Inspector-General as evidence of merit of Capt. Mosby.

R. E. LEE,
General.

CHAPTER III.

AFTER the battle of Fredericksburg, in Decem-
ber, 1862, there was a lull in the storm of war.
The men on the outposts along the Rappahannock
had a sort of truce to hostilities, and began swapping
tobacco and coffee, just as the soldiers of Wellington
and Soult, on the eve of a great battle, filled their
canteens from the same stream.   At that time,
Stuart determined to make a Christmas raid about
Dumfries, which was on Hooker's line of communication with Washington.   I went with him.   He got
many prisoners, and wagons loaded with bon-bons
and all the good things of the festive season.   It
made us happy, but almost broke the sutlers' hearts.
A regiment of Pennsylvania cavalry left their camp
on the Occoquan, and their Christmas turkeys, and
came out to look for us.   They had better have
stayed at home; for all the good they did was to
lead Stuart's cavalry into their camp as they ran
through it.   After leaving Dumfries, Stuart asked
me to take Beattie and go on ahead.   The road ran
through a dense forest, and there was danger of an

ambuscade, of which every soldier has a horror who has read of Braddock's defeat. Beattie and I went forward at a gallop, until we met a large body of cavalry. As no support was in sight, several officers made a dash at us, and at the same time opened such a fire as to show that peace on earth and good will to men, which the angels and morning stars had sung on that day over 1800 years ago, was no part of their creed. The very fact that we did not run away ought to have warned them that somebody was behind us. When the whole body had got within a short distance of us, Stuart, who had heard the firing, came thundering up with the 1st Virginia cavalry. All the fun was over with the Pennsylvanians then. There was no more merry Christmas for them. Wade Hampton was riding by the side of Stuart. He went into the fight and fought like a common (or, rather, an uncommon) trooper. The combat was short and sharp, and soon became a rout; the Federal cavalry ran right through their camp, and gave a last look at their turkeys as they passed. But alas! they were "grease, but living grease no more" for them. There was probably some method in their madness in running through their camp. They calculated, with good reason, that the temptation would stop the pursuit.

A few days ago I read, in a book giving the history of the telegraph in the war, the despatch sent to Washington by the operator near there : "The 17th Pennsylvania cavalry just passed here, furiously charging to the rear." When we got to Burke's Station, on the Orange and Alexandria Railroad, while his command was closing up, Stuart put his own operator in charge of the instrument, and listened to a telegraphic conversation between the general commanding at Fairfax Court-House and the authorities at Washington. In order to bewilder and puzzle them, he sent several messages, which put them on a false scent. Just before leaving, he sent a message to Quartermaster-General Meigs, complaining of the inferior quality of the mules recently furnished by him. The wire was then cut. Having learned by the telegraph that Fairfax Court-House was held by a brigade of infantry, Stuart marched around north of it, and went into Loudoun — a land flowing with plenty. He made his headquarters at Col. Rogers's, near Dover, and rested until the next day. On the morning he left, I went to his room, and asked him to let me stay behind for a few days with a squad of men. I thought I could do something with them. He readily assented. I got nine men — including, of course, Beattie — who volunteered to go with me. This was the beginning of my career as a partisan. The work I accomplished in two or three days with this squad induced him to let me have a larger force to try my fortune. I took my men down into Fairfax, and in two days captured twenty cavalrymen, with their horses, arms, and equipments. I had the good luck, by mere chance, to come across a forester named John Underwood, who knew every rabbit-path in the county. He was a brave soldier, as well as a good guide. His death a few months afterward, at the hands of a deserter from our own army, was one of the greatest losses I sustained in the war. I dismounted to capture one of the picket posts, who could be seen by the light of their fire in the woods. We walked up within a few yards of it. The men, never suspecting danger, were absorbed in a game of euchre. I halted, and looked on for a minute or two, for I hated to spoil their sport. At last I fired a shot, to let them know that their relief had come. Nobody was hurt ; but one fellow was so much frightened that he nearly jumped over the tops of the trees.

They submitted gracefully to the fate of war. I made them lie down by a fence, and left a mounted man to stand guard over them while I went to capture another post about two miles off. These were Vermont cavalry, and being from the land of steady habits did not indulge in cards like their New York

friends, whom I had just left in the fence corner.
I found them all sound asleep in a house, except the
sentinel. Their horses were tied to the trees around
it. The night was clear and crisp and cold. As we
came from the direction of their camp, we were mistaken for the patrol until we got upon them. The
challenge of the sentinel was answered by an order
to charge, and it was all over with the boys from the
Green Mountains. Their surprise was so great that
they forgot that they had only pistols and carbines.
If they had used them, being in a house, they might
have driven us off. They made no resistance. The
next day I started back to rejoin Stuart, who was
near Fredericksburg. I found him in his tent, and
when I reported what I had done, he expressed great
delight. So he agreed to let me go back with fifteen
men and try my luck again. I went and never
returned. I was not permitted to keep the men
long. Fitz Lee complained of his men being with
me, and so I had to send them back to him. But
while I had them I kept things lively and humming.
I made many raids on the cavalry outposts, capturing
men, arms, and horses. Old men and boys had
joined my band. Some had run the gauntlet of
Yankee pickets, and others swam the Potomac to get
to me. Most men love the excitement of fighting,
but abhor the drudgery of camps. I mounted, armed

and equipped my command at the expense of the United States government. There was a Confederate hospital in Middleburg, where a good many wounded Confederate soldiers had been left during our Maryland campaign a few months before. These were now convalescent. I utilized them. They would go down to Fairfax on a raid with me, and then return to the hospital. When the Federal cavalry came in pursuit, they never suspected that the cripples they saw lying on their couches or hobbling about on crutches were the men who created the panic at night in their camps. At last I got one of the cripples killed, and that somewhat abated their ardor.

There are many comic as well as tragic elements that fill up the drama of war. One night I went down to Fairfax to take a cavalry picket. When I got near the post I stopped at the house of one Ben Hatton. I had heard that he had visited the picket post that day to give some information to them about me. I gave him the choice of Castle Thunder or guiding me through the pines to the rear of the picket.

Ben did not hesitate to go with me. Like the Vicar of Bray, he was in favor of the party in power. There was a deep snow on the ground, and when we got in sight of the picket fire, I halted and dismounted my men. As Ben had done all I wanted of him, and was a non-combatant, I did not want to expose him to the risk of getting shot, and so I left him with a man named Gall (generally called "Coonskin," from the cap he wore), and Jimmie, an Irishman, to guard our horses, which we left in the pines. With the other men, I went to make the attack on foot. The snow being soft, we made no noise, and had them all prisoners almost before they got their eyes open. But just then a fusilade was opened in the rear, where our horses were. Leaving a part of my men to bring on the prisoners, we mounted the captured horses and dashed back to the place where I had dismounted, to meet what I supposed was an attempt of the enemy to make a reprisal on me. When I got there I found Ben Hatton lying in a snowbank, shot through the thigh, but Jimmy and Coonskin had vanished. All that Ben knew was that he had been shot; he said that the Yankees had attacked their party, but whether they had carried off Jimmie and Coonskin, or Jimmie and Coonskin had carried them, he couldn't tell. What made the mystery greater was that all our horses were standing just as we left them, including the two belonging to the missing men. With our prisoners and spoil, we started home, Ben Hatton riding behind one of the men. Ben had lost a good deal of blood, but he man-

aged to hold on.   When we got into the road we met
a body of Wyndham's cavalry coming up to cut us
off.   They stopped and opened fire on us.   I knew
this was a good sign, and that they were not coming
to close quarters in the dark.   We went on by them.
By daybreak I was twenty miles away.   As soon as
it was daylight, Wyndham set out full speed up the
pike to catch me.   He might as well have been
chasing the silver-footed antelope,

> That gracefully and gayly springs,
> As o'er the marble courts of kings.

I was at a safe distance before he started.   He got
to Middleburg during the day, with his horses all
jaded and blown.   He learned there that I had
passed through about the dawn of day.   He returned
to camp with the most of his command leading their
broken-down horses.   In fact, his pursuit had done
him more damage than my attack.   He was an English officer, trained in the cavalry schools of Europe ;
but he did not understand such business.   This
affair was rather hard on Ben Hatton.   He was the
only man that got a hurt ; and that was all he got.
As it was only a flesh wound, it healed quickly ; but,
even if he had died from it, fame would have denied
her requiem to his name.   His going with me had
been as purely involuntary as if he had been carried

out with a halter round his neck to be hanged. I left him at his house, coiled up in bed, within a few hundred yards of the Yankee pickets. He was too close to the enemy for me to give him any surgical assistance; and he had to keep his wound a profound secret in the neighborhood, for fear the Yankees would hear of it and how he got it. If they had ever found it out, Ben's wife would have been made a widow. In a day or so, Coonskin and Jimmie came in, but by different directions. We had given them up for lost. They trudged on foot through the snow all the way up from Fairfax. Neither one knew that Ben Hatton had been shot. Each one supposed that all the others were prisoners, and he the only one left to tell the tale of the disaster. Both firmly believed that they had been attacked by the enemy, and, after fighting as long as Sir John Falstaff did by Shrewsbury clock, had been forced to yield; but they could not account for all our horses being where we left them. The mistakes of the night had been more ludicrous than any of the incidents of Goldsmith's immortal comedy, " She Stoops to Conquer." By a comparison of the statements of the three, I found out that the true facts were these: In order to keep themselves warm, they had walked around the horses a good deal and got separated Coonskin saw Jimmie and Ben Hatton moving about in the shadow of a tree, and took them to be Yankees. He immediately opened on them, and drew blood at the first fire. Hatton yelled and fell. Jimmie, taking it for granted that Coonskin was a Yankee, returned his fire; and so they were dodging and shooting at each other from behind trees, until they saw us come dashing up. As we had left them on foot a short while before, it never occurred to them that we were coming back on the captured horses. After fighting each other by mistake and wounding Ben Hatton, they had run away from us. It was an agreeable surprise to them to find that I had their horses. Ben Hatton will die in the belief that the Yankees shot him; for I never told him any better. I regret that historical truth forbids my concluding this comedy according to the rules of the drama — with a marriage.

FAUQUIER COUNTY, VA., Feb. 28, 1863.

GENERAL: — I have the honor to report, that at four o'clock on the morning of the 26th instant I attacked and routed, on the Ox road, in Fairfax, about two miles from Germantown, a cavalry outpost, consisting of a lieutenant and fifty men. The enemy's loss was one lieutenant and three men killed, and five captured; number of wounded not known; also thirty-nine horses, with all their accoutrements, brought off. There were also three horses killed.

I did not succeed in gaining the rear of the post, as I expected, having been discovered by a vidette when several hundred yards off, who fired, and gave the alarm, which compelled me to charge them in front. In the terror and confusion occasioned by our terrific yells, the most of them saved themselves by taking refuge in a dense thicket, where the darkness effectually concealed them. There was also a reserve of one hundred men half a mile off who might come to the rescue. Already encumbered with prisoners and horses, we were in no condition for fighting. I sustained no loss. The enemy made a small show of fight, but quickly yielded. They were in log houses, with the chinking knocked out, and ought to have held them against a greatly superior force, as they all had carbines.

My men behaved very gallantly, although mostly raw recruits. I had only twenty-seven men with me. I am still receiving additions to my numbers.

If you would let me have some of the dismounted men of the First Cavalry, I would undertake to mount them. I desire some written instructions from you with reference to exportation of products within the enemy's lines. I wish the bearer of this to bring back some ammunition, also some large-size envelopes and blank paroles.

I have failed to mention the fact the enemy pursued me as far as Middleburg, without accomplishing anything, etc. . . .

JNO. S. MOSBY.

Maj.-Gen. J. E. B. Stuart.

FAIRFAX COURT HOUSE, Jan. 27, 1863.

SIR :—Last night my pickets were driven in by some of Stuart's cavalry, wounding one and capturing nine. I then started with some two hundred men in pursuit.

Some twenty-seven miles beyond my pickets at Middleburg, I came up with them, and after a short skirmish, captured twenty-four of them. I have just returned.

P. WYNDHAM.

CAPT. CARROLL H. PORTER,
    Assistant Adjutant-General.

CHAPTER IV.

IT was the latter part of January, 1863, when I crossed the Rappahannock into Northern Virginia, which from that time until the close of the war was the theatre on which I conducted partisan operations. The country had been abandoned to the occupation of the Federal army the year before, when Johnston retired from Centreville, and had never been held by us afterward, except during the short time when the Confederate army was passing through in Gen. Lee's first campaign into Maryland. I told Stuart that I would, by incessant attacks, compel the enemy either greatly to contract his lines or to reinforce them; either of which would be of great advantage to the Southern cause. The means supplied me were hardly adequate to the end I proposed, but I thought that zeal and celerity of movement would go far to com· pensate for the deficiency of my numbers. There was a great stake to be won, and I resolved to play a bold game to win it. I think that Stuart was the only man in the army of Northern Virginia, except two or three who accompanied me and knew me well, who expected that I would accomplish anything. Other detachments of cavalry had been sent there at different times that had done little or nothing.

Nearly every one thought that I was starting out on a quixotic enterprise, that would result in doing no harm to the enemy, but simply in getting all of my own men killed or captured. When at last I secured an independent command, for which I had so longed, I was as happy as Columbus when he set forth from the port of Palos with the three little barks Isabella had given him to search for an unknown continent. My faith was strong, and I never for a moment had a feeling of discouragement or doubted my ability to reap a rich harvest from what I knew was still an ungleaned field. I stopped an hour or so at Warrenton, which has always been a sort of political shrine from which the Delphian Apollo issues his oracles. After the war I made it my home, and it is generally supposed that I resided there before the war; the fact is that I never was in that section of Virginia until I went there as a soldier. The Union soldiers knew just as much about the country as I did.

I recall vividly to mind the looks of surprise and the ominous shaking of the heads of the augurs when I told them that I proposed going farther North to begin the war again along the Potomac. Their criticism on my command was pretty much the same as that pronounced on the English mission to Cabul some years ago — that it was too small for an army and too large for an embassy.

When I bade my friends at the Warren-Green Hotel "good-by," I had their best wishes for my success, but nothing more. They all thought that I was going on the foolhardy enterprise of an Arctic voyager in search of the North Pole. My idea was to make the Piedmont region of the country lying between the Rappahannock and Potomac Rivers the base of my operations. This embraces the upper portion of the counties of Fauquier and Loudoun. It is a rich, pastoral country, which afforded subsistence for my command, while the Blue Ridge was a safe point to which to retreat if hard pressed by the superior numbers that could be sent against us. It was inhabited by a highly refined and cultivated population, who were thoroughly devoted to the Southern cause. Although that region was the Flanders of the war, and harried worse than any of which history furnishes an example since the desolation of the Palatinates by Louis XIV.,[1] yet the stubborn faith

---

[1] [*Telegram.*]

KERNSTOWN, VA., Nov. 26, 1864.

SHERIDAN TO HALLECK : — " I will soon commence work on Mosby. Heretofore I have made no attempt to break him up, as I would have employed ten men to his one, and for the reason that I have made

of the people never wavered. Amid fire and sword they remained true to the last, and supported me through all the trials of the war. While the country afforded an abundance of subsistence, it was open and scant of forests, with no natural defensive advantages for repelling hostile incursions. There was no such shelter there as Marion had in the swamps of the Pedee, to which he retreated. It was always my policy to avoid fighting at home as much as possible, for the plain reason that it would have encouraged an overwhelming force to come again, and that the services of my own command would have been neutralized by the force sent against it. Even if I defeated them, they would

a scapegoat of him for the destruction of private rights. Now there is going to be an intense hatred of him in that portion of the valley which is nearly a desert. I will soon commence on Loudoun County, and let them know there is a God in Israel. Mosby has annoyed me considerably; but the people are beginning to see that he does not injure me a great deal, but causes a loss to them of all that they have spent their lives in accumulating. Those people who live in the vicinity of Harper's Ferry are the most villanous in this valley, and have not yet been hurt much. If the railroad is interfered with, I will make some of them poor. Those who live at home in peace and plenty want the duello part of this war to go on; but when they have to bear the burden by loss of property and comforts, they will cry for peace." When Sheridan started in March, 1865, from Winchester, to join Grant in front of Petersburg, he left my command behind him, more flourishing than it ever had been. The "*intense hatred*" he had hoped to excite in the people of the valley for me, by burning their homes, was only felt for him. They were not willing that I should be a scapegoat to bear another's sins.

return with treble numbers. On the contrary, it was safer for me, and greater results could be secured, by being the aggressor and striking the enemy at unguarded points. I could thus compel him to guard a hundred points, while I could select any one of them for attack. If I could do so, I generally slipped over when my territory was invaded and imitated Scipio by carrying the war into the enemy's camps.

I have seen it stated in the reports of some Federal officers that they would throw down the gage of battle to me in my own country and that I would not accept it. I was not in the habit of doing what they wanted me to do. Events showed that my judgment was correct. After I had once occupied I never abandoned it, although the wave of invasion several times rolled over it.

News of the surrender, or, rather, the evacuation, of Richmond came to me one morning in April, 1865, at North Fork, in Loudoun County, where my command had assembled to go on a raid. Just two or three days before that I had defeated Colonel Reno, with the Twelfth Pennsylvania Cavalry, at Hamilton, a few miles from there, which was the last fight in which I commanded. Reno afterward enjoyed some notoriety in connection with the Custer massacre. My purpose was to weaken the armies invading Virginia, by harassing their rear. As a line is only as strong as its weakest point, it was necessary for it to be stronger than I was at every point, in order to resist my attacks. It is easy, therefore, to see the great results that may be accomplished by a small body of cavalry moving rapidly from point to point on the communications of an army. To destroy supply trains, to break up the means of conveying intelligence, and thus isolating an army from its base, as well as its different corps from each other, to confuse their plans by capturing despatches, are the objects of partisan war. It is just as legitimate to fight an enemy in the rear as in front. The only difference is in the danger. Now, to prevent all these things from being done, heavy detachments must be made to guard against them. The military value of a partisan's work is not measured by the amount of property destroyed, or the number of men killed or captured, but by the number he keeps watching. Every soldier withdrawn from the front to guard the rear of an army is so much taken from its fighting strength.

I endeavored, as far as I was able, to diminish this aggressive power of the army of the Potomac, by compelling it to keep a large force on the defensive. I assailed its rear, for there was its most vulnerable point. My men had no camps. If they had gone into camp, they would soon have all been captured. They would scatter for safety, and gather at my call, like the Children of the Mist. A blow would be struck at a weak or unguarded point, and then a quick retreat. The alarm would spread through the sleeping camp, the long roll would be beaten or the bugles would sound to horse, there would be mounting in hot haste and a rapid pursuit. But the partisans generally got off with their prey. Their pursuers were striking at an invisible foe. I often sent small squads at night to attack and run in the pickets along a line of several miles. Of course, these alarms were very annoying, for no human being knows how sweet sleep is but a soldier. I wanted to use and consume the Northern cavalry in hard work. I have often thought that their fierce hostility to me was more on account of the sleep I made them lose than the number we killed and captured. It has always been a wonder with people how I managed to collect my men after dispersing them. The true secret was that it was a fascinating life, and its attractions far more than counterbalanced its hardships and dangers. They had no camp duty to do, which, however necessary, is disgusting to soldiers of high spirit. To put them to such routine work is pretty much like hitching a race-horse to a plow.

Many expeditions were undertaken and traps laid

to capture us, but all failed, and my command continued to grow and flourish until the final scene at Appomattox. It had just reached its highest point of efficiency when the time came to surrender. We did not go into a number of traps set to catch us, but somehow we always brought the traps off with us. One stratagem was after the model of the Grecian horse, and would have done credit to Ulysses. They sent a train of wagons up the Little River turnpike from Fairfax, apparently without any guard, thinking that such a bait would surely catch me. But in each wagon were concealed six of the Bucktails, who would, no doubt, have stopped my career, if I had given them a chance. Fortunately, I never saw them, for on that very day I had gone by another route down to Fairfax. When the Bucktails returned, they had the satisfaction of knowing that I had been there in their absence. At that time Hooker's army was in winter quarters on the Rappahannock, with a line of communication with Washington, both by land and water. The troops belonging to the defences at Washington were mostly cantoned in Fairfax, with their advance post at Centreville. West of the Blue Ridge, Milroy occupied Winchester. From my rendezvous east of the ridge I could move on the radius and strike any point on the circumference of the circle which was not too strongly guarded. But if I compelled them to be stronger everywhere than I was, then so much the better. I had done my work. Panics had often occurred in the camp when we were not near; the pickets became so nervous, expecting attacks, that they fired at every noise. It was thought that the honor as well as the safety of the army required that these depredations should no longer be endured, and that something must be done to stop them. Of course, the best way to do it was to exterminate the band, as William of Orange did the Macdonald of Glencoe. A cavalry expedition, under a Major Gilmer, was sent up to Loudoun to do the work. He had conceived the idea that I had my head-quarters in Middleburg, and might be caught by surrounding the place in the night-time. He arrived before daybreak, and threw a cordon of pickets around it. At the dawn of day he had the village as completely invested as Metz was by the Germans. He then gradually contracted his lines, and proceeded in person to the hotel where he supposed I was in bed. I was not there; I never had been. Soldiers were sent around to every house with orders to arrest every man they could find. When he drew in his net there was not a single soldier in it He had, however, caught a number of old men. It was a frosty morning, and he amused himself by making a soldier take them through a squad drill to keep them warm; occasionally he would make them mark time in the street front of the hotel. All this afforded a good deal of fun to the major, but was rather rough on the old men. He thought, or pretended to think, that they were the parties who had attacked his pickets. After a night march of twenty-five miles, he did not like to return to camp without some trophies, so he determined to carry the graybeards with him. He mounted each one behind a trooper, and started off. Now, it so happened that I had notified my men to meet that morning at Rector's Cross Roads, which is about four miles above Middleburg. When I got there I heard that the latter place was occupied by Federal cavalry. With seventeen men I started down the pike to look after them. Of course, with my small force, all that I could expect to do was to cut off some straggling parties who might be marauding about the neighborhood. When I got near Middleburg I learned that they had gone. We entered the town at a gallop. The ladies all immediately crowded around us. There were, of course, no men among them; Major Gilmer had taken them with him. There was, of course, great indignation at the rough usage they had received, and their wives never expected to see them again. And then, to add to the pathos of the scene, were the tears and lamentations of the daughters. There were many as pure and as bright as any pearl that ever shone in Oman's green water. Their beauty had won the hearts of many of my men. To avenge the wrongs of distressed damsels is one of the vows of knighthood; so we spurred on to overtake the Federal cavalry, in hopes that by some accident of war we might be able to liberate the prisoners.

CHAPTER V.

" Still o'er these scenes my memory wakes,
    And fondly broods with miser care !
  Time but the impression stronger makes,
    As streams their channels deeper wear." — *Burns.*

ABOUT five miles below Middleburg is the vil·
    lage of Aldie, where I expected that the
Federal cavalry would halt. But when I got within
a mile of it I met a citizen, just from the place, who
told me the cavalry had passed through. With five
or six men I rode forward while the others followed
on more slowly. Just as I rose to the top of the hill
on the outskirts of the village, I suddenly came upon
two Federal cavalrymen ascending from the opposite
side. Neither party had been aware of the approach
of the other, and our meeting was so unexpected
that our horses' heads nearly butted together before
we could stop. They surrendered, of course, and
were sent to the rear. They said that they had been
sent out as videttes. Looking down the hill, I saw
before me several mounted men in the road, whom I
took to be a part of the rear-guard of Major Gilmer's

column. We dashed after them. I was riding a
splendid horse — a noble bay — Job's war-horse was
a mustang compared to him — who had now got his
mettle up and carried me at headlong speed right
among them. I had no more control over him than
Mazeppa had over the Ukraine steed to which he was
bound. I had scarcely started in the charge, before
I discovered that there was a body of cavalry dismounted at a mill near the roadside, which I had not
before seen. They were preparing to feed their
horses. As their pickets had given no alarm, they
had no idea that an enemy was near, and were stunned
and dazed by the apparition of a body of men who
they imagined must have dropped from the clouds
upon them. The fact was that we were as much
surprised as they were. I was unable to stop my
horse when I got to them, but he kept straight on
like a streak of lightning. Fortunately, the dismounted troopers were so much startled that it never
occurred to them to take a shot at me *in transitu.*
They took it for granted that an overwhelming force
was on them, and every man was for saving himself.
Some took to the Bull Run mountain, which was
near by, and others ran into the mill and buried
themselves like rats in the wheat bins. The mill
was grinding, and some were so much frightened
that they jumped into the hoppers and came near

being ground up into flour. When we pulled them
out there was nothing blue about them.

As I have stated, my horse ran with me past
the mill. My men stopped there and went to work,
but I kept on. And now another danger loomed
up in front of me. Just ahead was the bridge over
Little River, and on the opposite bank I saw another body of cavalry looking on in a state of bewildered excitement. They saw the stampede at
the mill and a solitary horseman, pistol in hand,
riding full speed right into their ranks. They never
fired a shot. Just as I got to the bridge I jumped
off my horse to save myself from capture; but just
at the same moment they wheeled and took to their
heels down the pike. They had seen the rest of
my men coming up. If I had known that they
were going to run I would have stayed on my horse.
They went clattering down the pike, with my horse
thundering after them. He chased them all the way
into the camp. They never drew rein until they
got inside their picket lines. I returned on foot to
the mill; not a half a dozen shots were fired. All
that couldn't get away surrendered. But just then
a Federal officer made his appearance at the bridge.
He had ridden down the river, and, having just
returned, had heard the firing, but did not comprehend the situation. Tom Turner of Maryland,

one of the bravest of my men, dashed at him. As Turner was alone, I followed him. I now witnessed a single-handed fight between him and the officer. For want of numbers, it was not so picturesque as the combat, described by Livy, between the Horatii and the Curatii, nor did such momentous issues depend upon it. But the gallantry displayed was equally as great. Before I got up I saw the horse of the Federal officer fall dead upon him, and at the same time Turner seemed about to fall from his horse. The Federal officer, who was Capt. Worthington of the Vermont cavalry, had fired while lying under his horse at Turner and inflicted quite a severe wound. The first thing Turner said to me was that his adversary had first surrendered, which threw him off his guard, and then fired on him. Worthington denied it, and said his shot was fired in fair fight. I called some of the men to get him out from under his horse. He was too much injured by the fall to be taken away, so I paroled and left him with a family there to be cared for. While all this was going on, the men were busy at the mill. They had a good deal of fun pulling the Vermont boys out of the wheat bins. The first one they brought out was so caked with flour that I thought they had the miller. We got the commanding officer, Capt. Huttoon, and ninteen men

and twenty-three horses, with their arms and equipments.   I lingered behind with one man, and sent
the captures back to Middleburg.   Now, all the
ladies there had been watching and listening as
anxiously to hear from us as Andromache and her
maids did for the news of the combat between Hector and Achilles.   Presently they saw a line of blue
coats coming up the pike, with some gray ones
mixed among them.   Then the last ray of hope
departed — they thought we were all prisoners, and
that the foe was returning to insult them.   One
of the most famous of my men — Dick Moran —
rode forward as a herald of victory.   He had the
voice of a fog horn, and proclaimed the glad tidings
to the town.   While I was still sitting on my horse
at the mill, three more of the Vermont men, thinking that all of us had gone, came out from their
hiding place.   I sent them on after the others.   Up
to this time I had been under the impression that
it was Maj. Gilmer's rear-guard that I had overtaken.   I now learned that this was a body of Vermont cavalry that had started that morning several
hours after Gilmer had left.   They had halted to
feed their horses at the mill.   As they came up
they had seen a body of cavalry turn off toward
Centreville.   That was all they knew.   I then rode
down the road to look after my horse that I had

lost. I had not gone far before I met the old men that Maj. Gilmer had taken off.

They were all happy at the ludicrous streak of fortune that had brought them deliverance. It seems that Maj. Gilmer knew nothing of the intention of Capt. Huttoon to pay Middleburg a visit that day. When he got below Aldie he saw a considerable body of cavalry coming from the direction of Fairfax. It never occurred to him that they were his own people. He took them for my men, and thought I was trying to surround him. Even if he did think the force he saw was my command, it is hard to understand why he should run away from the very thing that he was in search of. But so he did. Just at the point where he was when he saw the Vermont men the pike crosses the old Braddock road. It is the same on which the British general marched with young George Washington to death and defeat on the Monongahela. Maj. Gilmer turned and started down the Braddock road at about the speed that John Gilpin rode to Edmonton on his wedding day. The ground was soft, and his horses sank knee deep in the mud at every jump. Of course, those broke down first that were carrying two. As he thought he was hard pressed, he kept on fast and furious, taking no heed of those he left on the roadside. It was necessary to sacrifice a part to save the rest. Long before he got to Centreville, about one-half of his horses were sticking in the mud, and all his prisoners had been abandoned. They had to walk home. Maj. Gilmer never came after me again. I heard that he resigned his commission in disgust, and, with Othello, "bade farewell to the big wars that make ambition virtue." There was rejoicing in Middleburg that evening; all ascribed to a special providence the advent of the Vermont cavalry just in time to stampede the New Yorkers, and make them drop their prisoners; and that my horse had run away, and carried me safely through the Vermont squadron. The miller, too, was happy, because I had appeared just in time to save his corn. At night, with song and dance, we celebrated the events, and forgot the dangers of the day.

HEADQUARTERS CAVALRY BRIGADE,
Fairfax Court-House, Va., March 3, 1863.

SIR : — By order of Col. R. B. Price, I directed, on the night of the 1st instant, a reconnoissance to go in direction of Aldie.

The officer who commanded this reconnoissance was Major Joseph Gilmer, of the Eighteenth Pennsylvania Cavalry. He had two hundred men. The orders to him were to proceed carefully, and send back couriers through the night with information whether they saw any enemy or not.

This last order was disobeyed. They were not to cross Cub Run until daylight, and then try and gain all information possible by flankers and small detached scouting parties.

Major Gilmer went to Middleburg, and, while returning, the videttes of the First Vermont Cavalry noticed a part of his advance and prepared to skirmish. The advance fell back toward Aldie. Major Gilmer, instead of throwing out a party to reconnoitre, turned off with nearly the whole of his command in the direction of Groveton, to gain Centreville. The horses returned exhausted from being run at full speed for miles. A few of Major Gilmer's men left his command and went along the Little River turnpike toward the Vermont detachment. They reported that the men seen were a part of a scouting party under Major Gilmer, and that no enemy were in Aldie. Capt. Huttoon then entered the town, and halted to have the horses fed near a mill. Immediately beyond was a rising ground which hid the guerillas. While the horses were unbridled and feeding, the surprise occurred. As both the officers have been captured, and as the detachment was not under my command, and is not attached to this brigade, I have no means of receiving any official or exact report from them, nor is there any one belonging to that detachment here. All men belonging to this detachment seem to have fought well; the enemy did not pursue them; they fell back in good order.

Major Gilmer, when he returned, was unable to make a report to Lieut.-Col. [John S.] Krepps, who during the time I was confined from sickness, had charge of the camp. I ordered Major Gilmer under arrest early this morning, and have sent to Col. R. B. Price charges, of which the annexed is a copy. Major Gilmer lost but one man, belonging to the

Fifth New York Cavalry, who was mortally wounded by the
enemy and afterwards robbed.   He was away from the command and on this side of Aldie, his horse having given out.
The enemy seemed to have been concealed along the line
of march and murdered this man, when returning, without
provocation.

I have the honor to be, very respectfully, your obedient
servant,

ROBT. JOHNSTONE,
Lieut.-Col. Commanding Cavalry Brigade.

CAPT. C. H. POTTER,
Assistant Adjutant-General.

GENERAL ORDERS, ⎱   WAR DEPARTMENT.
            ⎰   ADJUTANT-GENERAL'S OFFICE.
No. 229. ⎰   *Washington, July* 23, 1863.

I. Before a General Court Martial, which convened in
the city of Washington, D. C., March 27, 1863, pursuant to
General Orders, No. 20, dated Headquarters Cavalry, Defences of Washington, near Fort Scott, Virginia, February
2, 1863, and Special Orders, No. 146, dated February 10,
1863 ; No. 150, dated February 16, 1863 ; No. 161, dated
March 6, 1863; and No. 164, dated March 21, 1863,
Headquarters Cavalry, Department of Washington, and of
which Colonel E. B. SAWYER, 1st Vermont Cavalry, is President, was arraigned and tried —

Major *Joseph Gilmer*, 18th Pennsylvania Cavalry.

CHARGE I. — " Drunkenness."

Specification — " In this ; that *Joseph Gilmer*, a Major of the
18th Pennsylvania Cavalry, he then being in the service of the United States, and while in command of
a reconnoitring party, on the second day of March,
1863, was so intoxicated from the effects of spirituous
liquors as to be incapacitated to perform his duties
in an officer-like manner. This at or near the village
of Aldie, in the State of Virginia."

CHARGE II. — " Cowardice."

Specification — " In this ; that *Joseph Gilmer*, a Major in the
18th Pennsylvania Cavalry, he then being in the service of the United States, upon the second day of
March, 1863, did permit and encourage a detachment of cavalry, in the service of the United States,
and under his command, to fly from a small body of
the 1st Vermont Cavalry, who were mistaken for the
enemy, without sending out any person or persons to
ascertain who they were, or what were their numbers ;
and that the said cavalry under his command, as
above stated, were much demoralized, and fled many
miles through the country in great confusion and
disorder. This near Aldie, in the State of Virginia."

To which charges and specifications the accused, Major
Joseph Gilmer, 18th Pennsylvania Cavalry, pleaded " Not
Guilty."

FINDING.

The Court, having maturely considered the evidence adduced, finds the accused, Major *Joseph Gilmer,* 18th Pennsylvania Cavalry, as follows : —

CHARGE I.

Of the *Specification,* " Guilty."
Of the CHARGE,   " Guilty."

CHARGE II.

Of the *Specification,* " Guilty."
Of the CHARGE,   " Not Guilty."

SENTENCE.

And the Court does therefore sentence him, Major *Joseph Gilmer,* 18th Pennsylvania Cavalry, " *To be cashiered.*"

II. The proceedings of the Court in the above case were disapproved by the Major-General commanding the Department of Washington, on account of fatal defects and irregularities in the record. But the testimony shows that the accused was *drunk* on duty, and brought disgrace upon himself and the service. The President directs that, as recommended by the Department Commander, he be dismissed the service ; and Major *Joseph Gilmer,* 18th Pennsylvania Cavalry, accordingly ceases to be an officer in the United States Service since the 20th day of July, 1863.

BY ORDER OF THE SECRETARY OF WAR :

E. D. TOWNSEND,
Assistant Adjutant-General.

FAIRFAX COURT HOUSE, March 2, 1863.

SIR : — Fifty men of the First Vermont Cavalry, from Companies H and M, under captains Huttoon and Woodward, were surprised in Aldie while feeding their horses by about 70 of the enemy. Both captains captured and about 15 men. They saw no enemy but the attacking party. Major Gilmer has returned with the scouting party that left last night. They were to Middleburg and saw but one rebel. I have anticipated the report of Lieutenant-Colonel Krepps, now in command, which will be forwarded in probably one hour.

ROBT. JOHNSTONE,
Lieutenant-Colonel, commanding Cavalry Brigade.

CAPT. C. H. POTTER,
Assistant Adjutant-General.

CHAPTER VI.

WITHIN a few weeks after I began operations in Northern Virginia, I received accessions to my command from various sources. I have before spoken of the convalescents in the hospital at Middleburg, out of whom I got some valuable service. The Confederate government did not furnish horses to the cavalry, but paid each man forty cents a day compensation for the use of his horse. When the trooper lost his horse, or it became disabled, he was given a furlough to go to get another. A great many of this class of men came to me, to whom I would furnish captured horses in consideration of their going with me on a few raids. I made a proposition to mount all the dismounted men of Fitz Lee's brigade in consideration of their serving with me a short time. It was declined, and they were sent over to Fauquier under command of an ambitious officer, who thought, like Sam Patch when he leaped over Genesee falls, that some things could be done as well as others. Reports of my forays, which had been almost uniformly successful, had spread through the army, and it seemed, after the thing had been done, to be a very easy thing to surprise and capture cavalry outposts. The result of this attempt at imitation was that all the dismounted men were returned as prisoners of war via Fort Monroe, the mounted officer who commanded them alone escaping capture.

About this time I received a valuable recruit in the person of Sergt. Ames of the 5th New York cavalry, who deserted his regiment to join me. I never really understood what his motives were in doing so. I never cared to inquire. The men of my command insisted that I should treat him simply as a prisoner, and send him back to join many of his comrades whom I had sent to Richmond. After a long conversation with him I felt an instinctive confidence in his sincerity. He came to me on foot, but proposed to return to camp and mount himself if I would receive him. It happened that a young man named Walter Frankland was present, who also came on foot to join my standard. With my consent they agreed to walk down to Fairfax that night, enter the cavalry camp on foot and ride out on two of the best horses they could find. At the same time, I started off on an expedition in another direction. I had not gone far before I struck the trail of a raiding party of cavalry that had been off into Loudoun committing depredations on the citizens. I met old Dr. Drake walking home through snow and mud knee deep. He told me that the Federal cavalry had met him in the road, while he was going around to attend to the sick, and had not only taken his horse but also his saddle-bags, with all his medicines. As the Confederacy was then in a state of blockade, medicine was more valuable than gold, and great suffering would be inflicted on a community by the loss even of Dr. Drake's small stock. He told us that the marauders were not far ahead, and we spurred on to overtake them. Fortunately, as they were not far from their camps, they deemed themselves safe, and scattered over the country a good deal.

Before going very far we overtook a party that had stopped to plunder a house. As they were more intent on saving their plunder than fighting, they scampered off, but we were close on their heels. We had intercepted them and were between them and their camp, so they had to run in an opposite direction. But very soon they came to a narrow stream, the Horsepen Run, which was booming with the melted snow. The man on the fleetest horse, who was some distance in advance of the others, plunged in and narrowly escaped being drowned. He was glad to get back even as a prisoner. The others did not care to follow his example, but quietly submitted to manifest destiny. We got them all. They were loaded down mostly with silver spoons, of which they had despoiled the houses they had visited. But the richest prize of all we got was old Dr. Drake's saddle-bags. I was strongly tempted to administer to each one of the prisoners a purge by way of making them expiate their offence. Now, when Dr. Drake parted with his saddle-bags, he never expected to see them again, and supposed that as long as the war lasted his occupation would be gone, as a doctor without medicine and implements of surgery is like a soldier without arms. His surprise and delight may be imagined when a few hours afterward his saddle-bags and the captured silver were brought to him to be restored to the owners.

We then proceeded on toward Fryingpan, where I had heard that a cavalry picket was stationed and waiting for me to come after them. I did not want them to be disappointed in their desire to visit Richmond. When I got within a mile of it and had stopped for a few minutes to make my disposition for attack, I observed two ladies walking rapidly toward me. One was Miss Laura Ratcliffe, a young lady to whom Stuart had introduced me a few weeks before, when returning from his raid on Dumfries — with her sister. Their home was near

Fryingpan, and they had got information of a plan
to capture me, and were just going to the house
of a citizen to get him to put me on my guard,
when fortune brought them across my path. But
for meeting them, my life as a partisan would have
closed that day. There was a cavalry post in sight
at Fryingpan, but near there, in the pines, a large
body of cavalry had been concealed. It was expected that I would attack the picket, but that my
momentary triumph would be like the fabled Dead
Sea's fruit — ashes to the taste — as the party in
the pines would pounce from their hiding-place upon
me.

A garrulous lieutenant had disclosed the plot to
the young lady, never dreaming that she would walk
through the snow to get the news to me. This was
not the only time during the war when I owed my
escape from danger to the tact of a Southern woman.
I concluded then to go in the direction of Dranesville
in search of game. When we reached Herndon Station,
I learned that the contents of a sutler's wagon, that
had broken down when passing there that day, were
concealed in a barn near by. The sutler had gone
into camp to get another team to haul his goods in.
In the exercise of our belligerent rights, we proceeded
to relieve him of any further trouble in taking care
of them. He had a splendid stock of cavalry boots,

with which he seemed to have been provided in anticipation of the wants of my men. Now, loaded down
with what was to us a richer prize than the Golden
Fleece, we started back, but could not forbear taking
along a cavalry picket near by which was not looking
for us, as it had been understood that we were to
attack Fryingpan that night, where preparations had
been made to receive us. Once more I had tempted
fortune, and from "the nettle danger had plucked the
flower safety."

On my return to Middleburg I found Ames and
Frankland there in advance of me. They had entered
the camp of the Fifth New York cavalry at night on
foot, and had ridden out on two of the finest horses
they could find in the stables. They had passed in
and out without ever having been molested or chal-
lenged by the guard. Ames had not had time to
exchange his suit of blue for a gray one, but Frankland was in full Confederate uniform. It was a perfectly legitimate enterprise, certainly, as open and
bold as the capture in the night-time of the Palladium
of Troy by Ulysses and Diomede. But still the men
were not satisfied of Ames's good faith. They said
that he had not betrayed Frankland because he
wanted to entrap us all at one time. A few days
after that, I once more put him to a test which convinced the men of his truth and fidelity. He seemed

to burn with an implacable feeling of revenge toward his old companions in arms. I never had a truer or more devoted follower. He was killed in a skirmish in October, 1864, and carried the secret of his desertion to the grave. I had made him a lieutenant, and he had won by his courage and general deportment the respect and affection of my men. They all sincerely mourned his death.

Since the war I have often passed his lonely grave in a clump of trees on the very spot where he fell. The soldier who killed him was in the act of taking his arms off when one of my men rode up and shot him. Ames is a prominent figure in the history of my command. It was my habit either to go myself, with one or two men, or to send scouts, to find out some weak and exposed place in the enemy's lines. I rarely rested for more than one day at a time. As soon as I knew of a point offering a chance for a successful attack, I gathered my men together and struck a blow. From the rapidity with which these attacks were delivered and repeated, and the distant points at which they were made, a most exaggerated estimate of the number of my force was made. I have before spoken of John Underwood, to whose courage and skill as a guide I was so much indebted for my earlier successes. He was equally at home threading a thick labyrinth of pines in Fairfax or

leading a charge. He was among the first everywhere, and I always rewarded his zeal. About this
time I had sent him down on a scout, from which he
returned informing me that a picket of thirty or forty
cavalry had been placed at Herndon Station on the
Loudoun & Hampshire Railroad. This was the very
place where I had got the sutler's wagon the week
before. I could hardly believe it — I thought it must
be another trap — for I could not imagine why such
a number of men should be put there, except for the
purpose of getting caught. I had supposed that the
enemy had been taught something by experience.
I collected my men and started down, though I did
not expect to find any one at Herndon when I got
there.

Fearing an ambuscade, and also hearing that the
reserve at the post stayed in a house, I thought I
would try my luck in the daytime. Besides, as most
of my attacks had been made at night, I knew they
would not expect me in the day. Underwood conducted me by all sorts of crooked paths through the
dense forests until we got in their rear. We then
advanced at a walk along the road leading to their
camp at Dranesville, until we came upon a vidette,
who saw us, but did not have time either to fire or to
run away. He was ours before he recovered his
senses, he was so much surprised. About 200 yards

in front of us, I could see the boys in blue lounging around an old sawmill, with their horses tied by their halters to the fence. It was past twelve o'clock, and the sun was shining brightly, but there was a deep snow on the ground. They were as unconscious of the presence of danger as if they had been at their own peaceful homes among the Green Mountains. It happened to be just the hour for the relief to come from their camp at Dranesville. They saw us approaching, but mistook us for friends. When we got within 100 yards, I ordered a charge. They had no time to mount their horses, and fled, panic-stricken, into the sawmill and took refuge on the upper floor. I knew that if I gave them time to recover from the shock of their surprise they could hold the mill with their carbines against my force until reenforcements reached them.

The promptness with which the opportunity was seized is the reason that they were lost and we were saved. They were superior in numbers, with the advantage of being under cover. The last ones had hardly got inside the mill before we were upon them. I dismounted and rushed into the mill after them, followed by John De Butts. The enemy were all above me. As I started up the steps I ordered the men to set fire to the mill. I knew that this order would be heard overhead and increase the panic. The mill was full of dry timber and shavings that would have burned them to cinders in ten minutes. As I reached the head of the stairway I ordered a surrender. They all did so. They had the alternative of doing this or being roasted alive. In a minute more the mill would have been in flames. Against such an enemy they had no weapon of defence, and, in preference to cremation, chose to be prisoners. On going out and remounting, I observed four finely caparisoned horses standing in front of the house of Nat Hanna, a Union man. I knew that the horses must have riders, and that from their equipments they must be officers. I ordered some of the men to go into the house and bring them out. They found a table spread with milk, honey, and all sorts of nice delicacies for a lunch. But no soldiers could be seen, and Mrs. Hanna was too good a Union woman to betray them. Some of the men went upstairs, but by the dim light could see nothing on the floor. Ames opened the door to the garret ; he peeped in and called, but it was pitch dark, and no one answered. He thought it would do no harm to fire a shot into the darkness. It had a magical effect. There was a stir and a crash, and instantly a human being was seen descending through the ceiling. He fell on the floor right among the men. The flash of the pistol in his face had caused him to change his position, and in doing so he had stepped on the lathing and fallen through. His descent had been easy and without injury to his person. He was thickly covered with lime dust and mortar. After he was brushed off, we discovered that we had a major. His three companions in the dark hole were a captain and two lieutenants, who came out through the trap-door, and rather enjoyed the laugh we had on the major. As we left the house the lunch disappeared with us. It was put there to be eaten. The major was rather dilatory in mounting. He knew that the relief was due there, and was in hope not only of a rescue, but of turning the tables and taking us with him to his camp. But fate had decreed otherwise. He was admonished of the importance of time to us, and that he must go right on to Richmond, where he had started to go the year before.

As soon as possible, John Underwood, with a guard, went on in advance with the prisoners. Just as we left the railroad station the relief appeared in sight. I remained behind with a dozen men as a rear-guard, to keep them back until Underwood had got far ahead. The relief party hung on in sight of me for some distance, but never attacked. After I crossed the Horsepen, which almost swam our horses, I started off at a gallop, thinking the pursuit was over. This emboldened the pursuers, and a few came on and crossed after me. I saw that they were divided, and I halted, wheeled, and started back at them. They did not wait for me, but got over the stream as fast as they could. One fellow got a good ducking. I was now master of the situation. I drew up on a hill and invited them to come across, but they declined. I was not molested any more that day. A rather ludicrous thing occurred when we made the attack at the station. There was a so-called Union man there, named Mayo Janney. As he lived just on the outskirts of the picket line, he was permitted to conduct a small store, and trade with Washington. He had been down to the city, and, with other things, had brought out a hogshead of molasses, which he intended to retail to his neighbors at speculative prices. The element of danger in such a trade was, of course, largely considered in estimating the market value of the merchandise. Janney had his store in the vacant railroad depot. He had just knocked out the bung of the barrel of molasses, and was in the act of drawing some to fill the jug of a customer, when he heard the clatter and yell of my men, as they rushed down on the terrified pickets. As Herndon Station and the region round about was supposed to be in the exclusive occupation of the

army of the United States, he could not have been
more surprised at an earthquake, or if a comet had
struck the earth.   Forgetting all about the molasses,
which he had left pouring out of the barrel, he
rushed wildly to the door to see what was the matter.   He saw the Vermont cavalry flying in every
direction in confusion, and whizzing bullets passing
unpleasantly close to his ears.   Now, to be a mar-
tyr in any cause was just the last thing which a
man in Fairfax, who had taken an oath to support
the constitution of the United States, had any idea
of being.   Janney's idea of supporting the Union
was to make some money out of it, and a living for
his family.   But he did not consider that his oath
required him to stay there to be shot, or to help
to bury or bind up the wounds of those who might
be.   His idea of honor was as selfish and material
as Sir John Falstaff's.   He preferred remaining a
live man without it, to being a dead one who died
with it yesterday.   So Janney ran away as fast as
his legs could carry him, and, if possible, his molasses ran faster than he did.   He did not return
for several hours to view the field.   When he at
last mustered up courage to go back, he found the
molasses about shoe-deep all over the floor, but not
a drop in the barrel.   Now, Janney's loyalty to the
Union was not altogether above suspicion.   It was

suspected that he had taken the oath for profit, and probably to enable him to act as a spy for me. The loss of his molasses proved his innocence ; but for that fact he would have been arrested and sent to board at the Old Capitol on the charge of having given me the information on which I had acted.

When I overtook my command at Middleburg, I found Dick Moran, after the style of the ancient bards, in the street, rehearsing the incidents of the day to an admiring crowd. I paroled the privates and let them go home, as I could not then spare a guard to take them back to the Confederate lines, which were at Culpepper. I put the four officers on their parole to report at Culpepper to Fitz Lee, and sent with them, simply as an escort, a Hungarian whom we called Jake. On the way out they spent one night at a farmer's house. Now, Jake had been a soldier under Kossuth, and having had some experience in Austrian perfidy, had no sort of confidence in the military value of a parole. When time came for the officers to go to bed, Jake volunteered to take their boots down to the kitchen to be blacked. He had no fears of their leaving, barefooted, in the snow, as long as he held on to their boots. Jake told me, with a chuckle, of his stratagem, on his return. He never doubted that it kept his prisoners from going away that night.

DRANESVILLE, VA., March 24, 1863.

COLONEL: — I have the honor to report, on the 17th instant, at 1 P.M., the reserve picket post at Herndon Station, consisting of twenty-five men, under command of Second Lieut. Alexander G. Watson, Company L, First Vermont Cavalry, was surprised by Capt. Mosby, with a force of forty-two men, and twenty-one of our men, together with Maj. William Wells, Capt. Robert Schofield, Company F, and Second Lieut. Alexander G. Watson, Company L, and Perley C. J. Cheney, Company C (second lieutenant) captured, all of First Vermont Cavalry; the three first were visiting the post. The surprise was so complete the men made but little or no resistance. The enemy were led on by citizens and entered on foot by a bridle-path in rear of the post, capturing the vidette stationed on the road before he was able to give the alarm. Every effort was made, on receipt of the intelligence by me, to capture the party, but without avail. Had Second Lieut. Edwin H. Higley, Company K, First Vermont Cavalry, who had started with the relief for the post, consisting of forty men, together with ten of the old guard, who joined him, performed his duty, the whole party could, and would, have been taken. I cannot too strongly urge that orders may be given that all citizens near outpost must remove beyond the lines. Such occurrences are exceedingly discreditable, but sometimes unavoidable, not only calculated to embolden the enemy, but dispirit our men. I am, &c.,

CHARLES F. TAGGART,
Major, Commanding Post.

COL. R. BUTLER PRICE,
Commanding, &c.

NEAR PIEDMONT, VA., March 18, 1863.

GENERAL : — Yesterday I attacked a body of the enemy's cavalry at Herndon Station, in Fairfax County, completely routing them. I brought off twenty-five prisoners — a major (Wells), one captain, two lieutenants, and twenty-one men, all their arms, twenty-six horses and equipments. One, severely wounded, was left on the ground. The enemy pursued me in force, but were checked by my rear-guard and gave up the pursuit. My loss was nothing.

The enemy have moved their cavalry from Germantown back of Fairfax Court House on the Alexandria pike.

In this affair my officers and men behaved splendidly, &c.

JNO. S. MOSBY,
Captain, &c.

[*Indorsement.*]

MAJ.-GEN. J. E. B. STUART.

HEADQUARTERS ARMY OF NORTHERN VIRGINIA,
March 21, 1863.

Respectfully forwarded for the information of the department and as evidence of the merit and continued success of Captain Mosby.

R. E. LEE,
General.

CHAPTER. VII.

*" 'Tis sweet to win, no matter how, one's laurels.
By blood or ink." — Don Juan.*

DURING the time I had been operating against
the outposts of the Union army in Northern
Virginia I kept up a regular correspondence with
Stuart by means of couriers, and reported to him the
result of every action. The base from where I oper-
ated was on its flank, and so I compelled it to present
a double front. The prisoners taken were sometimes
released on their paroles, but generally sent out
under charge of a guard to the provost marshal at
Culpepper Court House. The necessity of making
the details for guard duty seriously diminished my
effective strength. It would take nearly a week for
them to go over and return, and I was often compelled to wait on that account before undertaking an
expedition. The men, too, who would join me to go
on a raid just to get a horse would generally quit as
soon as it was over to return to their own regiments.
When an enterprise had been accomplished, I was
often left as forlorn as Montrose after fighting and

winning a battle with the undisciplined Highland clans — they had all scattered and gone home with their plunder. I would have to give notice of my place and time of meeting several days in advance, in order to make sure of a sufficient number answering the call to effect any good work. The longer I remained in the country, successful raids became more difficult, as the enemy was all the time on the lookout, and kept every point closely guarded. I had promised Stuart, as an inducement to let me have some men, either to compel the enemy to contract their lines in Fairfax County or to reinforce them heavily. Having no fixed lines to guard or defined territory to hold, it was always my policy to elude the enemy when they came in search of me, and carry the war into their own camps.

This was the best way to keep them at home. To have fought my own command daily, on equal terms and in open combats against the thousands that could have been brought against it by the North, would soon have resulted in its entire annihilation. I endeavored to compensate for my limited resources by stratagems, surprises, and night attacks, in which the advantage was generally on my side, notwithstanding the superior numbers we assailed. For this reason, the complaint has often been made against me that I would not fight fair. So an old Austrian

general complained that Bonaparte violated all military maxims and traditions by flying about from post
to post in Italy, breaking up his cantonments and
fighting battles in the winter time. The accusations
that have been made against my mode of warfare are
about as reasonable. In one sense the charge that
I did not fight fair is true. I fought for success and
not for display. There was no man in the Confederate army who had less of the spirit of knight-
errantry in him, or took a more practical view of war
than I did. The combat between Richard and
Saladin by the Diamond of the Desert is a beautiful
picture for the imagination to dwell on, but it isn't
war, and was no model for me. The poets have
invested the deeds of the Templars with the colors
of romance; but if they were half as generous as
they were said to have been, it was because their
swords, and not their hearts, were dedicated to a
cause.

I never admired and did not imitate the example
of the commander who declined the advantage of the
first fire. But, while I conducted war on the theory
that the end of it is to secure peace by the destruction of the resources of the enemy, with as small
a loss as possible to my own side, there is no authen-
ticated act of mine which is not perfectly in accordance with approved military usage. Grant, Sheridan,

and Stonewall Jackson had about the same ideas
that I had on the subject of war. I will further add
that I was directly under the orders of Stuart up to
the time of his death, in May, 1864, and after that
time, of Gen. Robert E. Lee, until the end of the
war. With both of these two great Christian
soldiers I had the most confidential relations. My
military conduct received from them not only appro-
bation, but many encomiums. In a letter received
from Stuart about this, he said, " I heartily wish you
great and increasing success in the glorious career
on which you have entered."

In September, 1864, I visited Gen. Lee at his
headquarters, near Petersburg. I had been badly
wounded a week or so before by a bullet, which
I still carry in me. When he saw me hobbling up
to him on my crutches, he came to meet me, and
said, as he extended his hand, " Colonel, I have
never had but one fault to find with you — you are
always getting wounded." I mention this circumstance to show that all I did had the sanction of the
commander of the army of Northern Virginia, of
which my own command — the Forty-third Battalion
of Virginia Cavalry — was a part. I was independent simply in the sense that both Gen. Lee and
Gen. Stuart had such confidence in me that they
never undertook to trammel me with orders, but

gave me full discretion to act as I chose. After the death of Stuart, Gen. Lee frequently wrote to me, although we were separated by a distance of over a hundred miles. All of his letters are in his own handwriting. What were called my depredations had caused another brigade of cavalry to be sent into Fairfax to protect Washington. The frequent incursions we had made down there created great alarm and an apprehension that they might be extended across the Potomac. The deliberations of the Senate were frequently disturbed by the cry that the Gauls were at the gate. One day I rode down on a scout in sight of the dome of the Capitol, when a wagon came along, going to Washington, which was driven by the wife of a Union man who had left his home in Virginia and taken refuge there. I stopped it, and, after some conversation with the driver, told her who I was. With a pair of scissors she had I cut off a lock of my hair and sent it to Mr. Lincoln, with a message that I was coming to get one of his soon. A few days after this, I saw in the *Star* that it had been delivered to him, and that the President enjoyed the joke.

After returning from my last expedition to Herndon Station, I had sent John Underwood down to search along the lines for a weak point where I might make a successful attack. This had now become very difficult to do. There had been so many real and false alarms that the pickets were always on the watch, and slept with their eyes open. The videttes were stationed so close together that it was impossible to pass them without being discovered ; and a snowbird could not fly by without being fired at. They had so strengthened their lines that, where formerly there had been not over a dozen men, there were now a hundred. If there was a hole anywhere, I knew that John Underwood would find it. I had about that time received another recruit, who became famous in the annals of my command. His home was in Loudoun, and his name was William Hibbs. He was always called the "Major," although he never held a commission. He was a blacksmith by trade, over fifty years old, and had already fully discharged the duty he owed to the Southern Confederacy by sending his two sons into the army. But for my appearance in the vicinity, he would probably have lived and died unheard.

The fame of the exploits of my men, and the rich prizes they won, aroused his martial ambition ; and he determined to quit the forge and become a warrior bold. The country soon echoed the notes of his fame, as the anvil had once rung with the strokes of his hammer. Around the triumvirate — Dick Moran, John Underwood, and Major Hibbs — recruits now

gathered as iron filings cluster around a magnet.
They were the germs from which my command grew
and spread like a banyan tree. Beattie, who was
always my faithful Achates, had been captured, but
was soon afterward exchanged. Underwood, on his
return from his scout, reported a body of about 100
cavalry at Chantilly, which was in supporting distance of several other bodies of about equal numbers. An attack on the post there would be
extremely hazardous, on account of the proximity
of the others. The chance of success was a poor
one; but, as about fifty men had assembled to go
with me, I did not like to disappoint them. Each
man wanted a horse, as well as a leader to show him
how to get one. They were all willing to risk a
good deal, and so was I. We started off for Chantilly, down the Little River Turnpike, as the mud
prevented our travelling any other route. The advantage of attacking at Chantilly was not only that
we had a good road to travel on, but I knew it was
the very last place they expected I would attack.
They did not look for my approach in broad daylight
along the pike, but thought I would come by some
crooked path after dark through the pines.

I had never asked a commission of the Confederate
government, but the warfare I had been conducting
had attracted the attention of Gen. Robert E. Lee,

who not only complimented me in general orders published to the army, but at his request the President of the Confederate States sent me a commission as captain, with authority to organize a company of cavalry. This was succeeded, in the course of two or three weeks, with a commission of major. Before the close of the war I became a full colonel, which was the highest rank I got. My first commission was accompanied by the following letter : —

HEADQUARTERS ARMY OF NORTHERN VIRGINIA,
March 23, 1863.

CAPT. J. S. MOSBY, *through Major-General Stuart.*

CAPTAIN : — You will perceive from the copy of the order herewith inclosed that the President has appointed you captain of partisan rangers. The general commanding directs me to say that it is desired that you proceed at once to organize your company, with the understanding that it is to be placed on a footing with all the troops of the line, and to be mustered unconditionally in the Confederate service for and during the war. Though you are to be its captain, the men will have the privilege of electing the lieutenants so soon as its members reach the legal standard. You will report your progress from time to time, and when the requisite number of men are enrolled, an officer will be designated to muster the company into the service.

I am, very respectfully, your obedient servant,

W. W. TAYLOR, *A. A. G.*

The partisan ranger law was an act of the Confederate Congress authorizing the President to issue commissions to officers to organize partisan corps. They stood on the same footing with other cavalry organizations in respect to rank and pay, but, in addition, were given the benefit of the law of maritime prize. There was really no novelty in applying this principle to land forces. England has always done so in her Majesty's East Indian service, and the spoils of Waterloo were divided among the captors, of which Wellington took his share. The booty of Delhi was the subject of litigation in the English Court of Chancery, and Havelock, Campbell and Outram returned home from the East loaded with barbaric spoils. As there is a good deal of human nature in people, and as Major Dalgetty is still the type of a class, it will be seen how the peculiar privileges given to my men served to whet their zeal. I have often heard them disputing over the division of the horses before they were captured, and it was no uncommon thing for a man to remind me just as he was about going into a fight that he did not get a horse from the last one. On the Chantilly raid I was accompanied by Captain Hoskins, an English officer, who had just reported to me with a letter from Stuart. He had been a captain in the English army and had won the Crimean medal. After the

conclusion of peace he had returned home, but dis-
liking the monotonous life of the barracks, had sold
his commission and joined Garibaldi in his Sicilian
expedition. He was a thorough soldier of fortune,
devoted to the profession of arms, and loved the
excitement of danger and the joy of battle. He had
been attracted to our shores by the great American
war, which offered a field for the display of his courage and the gratification of his military tastes. He
was a noble gentleman and a splendid soldier, but his
career with me was short. A few weeks after that
he fell fighting by my side.

I mounted Hoskins and his companion, Captain
Kennon, on captured horses, and they went to try
their luck with me. The post at Chantilly was only
two miles from the camp of a division of cavalry,
and flanked by strong supporting parties on each
side. When I got within two or three miles of it,
I turned obliquely off to the right, in order to penetrate, if possible, between them and Centreville, and
gain their rear. But they were looking out for me,
and I found there was no chance for a surprise. I
despaired almost of doing anything; but as I did
not want to go back without trying to do something, I ordered a few men to chase in the pickets,
in hopes that this would draw their main body out
for some distance. They did so, and several were

killed and captured.   From a high position I saw
the reserve mount, form, and move up the pike.   I
regained the pike also, so as not to be cut off.   I
got ready to charge as soon as they were near, although I did not have half their number, when I
discovered another large body of cavalry, that had
heard the firing, coming rapidly from the direction
of Fryingpan to reinforce them.   These were more
than I had bargained to fight in the open, so I ordered a retreat at a trot up the turnpike.   I was
certain that they would pursue rapidly, thinking I
was running away, and, getting strung out along
the pike, would lose their advantage in numbers, and
give me a chance to turn and strike back.   My calculation was right.   I kept my men well closed up,
with two some distance behind, to give me notice
when they got near.   I had just passed over a hill,
and was descending on the other side, when one of
my men dashed up and said the enemy was right
upon me.   I looked back, but they were not in
sight.   I could distinctly hear their loud cheers and
the hoofstrokes of their horses on the hard pike.
I had either to suffer a stampede or make a fight.
The cavalry officer is like the woman who deliber-
ates — he's lost.   If I had gone a step further my
retreat would have degenerated into a rout.

My horses were jaded by a long day's march,

while the enemies' were fresh. I promptly ordered the men to halt, right about wheel, and draw sabres. It was all done in the twinkling of an eye. Fortunately, just at the place where I halted was an abattis, formed of fallen trees, which had been made by the army the year before. The men formed behind these, as I knew that when they darted out it would create the impression on my pursuers that I had drawn them into an ambuscade. As they stood there, calmly waiting for me to give the word for the onset,

> A horrid front they form,
> Still as the breeze, but dreadful as the storm.

I had no faith in the sabre as a weapon. I only made the men draw their sabres to prevent them from wasting their fire before they got to closer quarters. I knew that when they got among them the pistol would be used. My success had been so uninterrupted that the men thought that victory was chained to my standard. Men who go into a fight under the influence of such feelings are next to invincible, and are generally victors before it begins. We had hardly got into position before the head of the pursuing column appeared over the hill, less than 100 yards off. They had expected to see our backs, and not our faces. It was a rule from which, during the war, I never departed, not to stand still and receive a charge, but always to act on the offensive. This was the maxim of Frederick the Great, and the key to the wonderful successes he won with his cavalry. At the order to charge, my men dashed forward with a yell that startled and stunned those who were foremost in pursuit. I saw them halt, and I knew then that they had lost heart and were beaten. Before they could wheel, my men were among them. Those who were coming up behind them, seeing those in front turn their backs, did the same thing. They had no idea they were running away from the same number of men they had been chasing. My men had returned their sabres to their scabbards, and the death-dealing revolver was now doing its work.

The Union cavalry had assumed, as I thought they would, that my retreat had only been feigned to draw them into a trap. They could not understand why I ran away just to run back again. They had no time to ascertain our numbers or to recover from the shock of their surprise in finding us drawn up to receive them. I never witnessed a more complete rout, or one with less cause for it. The chase continued two or three miles. It was almost dark when we stopped. I remember that in the first set of fours that led the charge were three young men, James W.

Poster, Thomas W. Richards, and William L. Hunter, to whom I gave commissions for their gallant conduct. They all have since won honorable positions in civil life. We left the killed and wounded on the field, brought off thirty-six prisoners and about fifty horses. By strategy and hard fighting, four times our numbers had been defeated. The only casualty in my command happened to Major Hibbs, who had his boot-heel shot off. He had been one of the foremost leaders in the charge, and like Byron's corsair, everywhere in the thickest of the fight "shone his mailed breast and flashed his sabre's ray." When the "Major" rode up to me, after the fight was over, he was almost a maniac, he was so wild with delight. And when, in the presence of all the men, I praised his valor, he could no longer contain himself; he laughed and wept by turns. All that he could say in reply was: "Well, Captain, I knew the work had to be done, and that was the way to do it." One thing is certain, the Major got a good horse as a reward. The regiment we had fought happened to be the very one to which Ames had belonged, and from which he had deserted a few weeks before to join me. He had gone through their ranks like an avenging angel, shooting right and left. He took a malicious pleasure in introducing some of his old comrades to me. I could not help feeling a pang of regret that such courage as his should be stained with dishonor. **It** was Hoskins's first fight with me. He said it was better than a fox chase. I recall his image now as it rises above the flood of years, as he hewed his path through the broken ranks. It was a point of honor or of military etiquette with him to use his sword and not his pistol. In this way he lost his life. I reported to Stuart the result of the engagement and received from him the following letter in reply:

HEADQUARTERS CAVALRY DIVISION,
ARMY OF NORTHERN VIRGINIA,
March 27, 1863.

CAPTAIN: — Your telegram announcing your brilliant achievement near Chantilly was duly received and forwarded to General Lee. He exclaimed upon reading it:

"Hurrah for Mosby! I wish I had a hundred like him."

Heartily wishing you continued success, I remain your obedient servant, J. E. B. STUART,
Major- General Commanding.

Captain J. S. MOSBY, *Commanding, etc.*

FAIRFAX COURT-HOUSE, March 23, 1863.

SIR: — At 5 P.M., our picket in front of Chantilly was attacked. The videttes were on the alert, and gave the alarm. The reserve of about 70 men were immediately under arms, and charged the enemy, who fled for 2 miles along the Little River turnpike. Between Saunder's toll-gate and Cub Run there is a strip of woods about a half a mile wide through which the road runs. Within the woods, and about a quarter of a mile apart, are two barricades of fallen trees; our troops pursued the enemy between these barricades. Behind the latter, some of the enemy were concealed. The head of the column was here stopped by a fire of carbines and pistols, and also by a fire upon the flank from the woods. The column broke, and was pursued by the enemy 1½ miles. It was then rallied by the exertions of Majors Bacon and White. Captains McGuinn and Hasbrouck, when they heard of the alarm, proceeded on a gallop from Fryingpan, and, joining Major White's command, pursued the enemy for 8 miles. Night coming on, and the enemy being more numerous than we were, and our horses exhausted, the column halted and returned to Chantilly. The line of pickets is now established. Our loss is, killed, Corporal Gilles, Company H. Fifth New York Cavalry; James Doyle, Company C; John Harris, Company L. Mortally wounded, Sergeant Leahey, Company C. Lieutenant Merritt taken prisoner.

ROBT. JOHNSTONE,
Lieutenant Colonel Commanding.

Col. R. Butler Price,
    Commanding Cav. Brig.

[*Indorsement.*]

Headquarters Army Northern Virginia,
March 26, 1863.

General : — On the 25th [23] instant Capt. Mosby attacked and routed a body of the enemy's cavalry on the Little River turnpike, near Chantilly. He reports 10 killed and wounded — and a lieutenant and 30 [35] men, with their horses, arms, and equipments captured. He sustained no loss. . . . etc.   R. E. LEE, *General.*

FAUQUIER COUNTY, VA., April 7, 1863.

GENERAL : — I have the honor to submit the following report of the operations of the cavalry under my command since rendering my last report. On Monday, March 16, I proceeded down the Little River pike to capture two outposts of the enemy, each numbering 60 or 70 men. I did not succeed in gaining their rear as I expected, and only captured 4 or 5 videttes. It being late in the evening, and our horses very much jaded, I concluded to return. I had gone not over a mile back when we saw a large body of the enemy's cavalry, which, according to their own reports, numbered 200 men, rapidly pursuing. I feigned a retreat, desiring to draw them off from their camps. At a point where the enemy had blockaded the road with fallen trees, I formed to receive them, for with my knowledge of the Yankee character I knew they would imagine themselves fallen into an ambuscade. When they had come within 100 yards of me I ordered a charge, to which my men responded with a vim that swept everything before them. The Yankees broke when we got in 75 yards of them ; and it was more of a chase than a fight for 4 or 5 miles. We killed 5, wounded a considerable number, and brought off 1 lieutenant and 35 men prisoners. I did not have over 50 men with me, some having gone back with the prisoners and others having gone on ahead, when we started back, not anticipating any pursuit. On Monday, March 31, I went down in the direction of Dranesville to capture several strong outposts in the vicinity of that place. On reaching there I discovered that they had fallen back about 10 miles down the Alexandria pike. I then returned 6 or 8 miles back and stopped about 10 o'clock at night at a point about 2 miles from the pike. Early the next morning one of my men, whom I had left over on the Leesburg pike, came dashing in, and announced the rapid approach of the enemy. But he had scarcely given us the information when the enemy appeared a few hundred yards off, coming up at a gallop. At this time our horses were eating; all had their bridles off, and some even their saddles — they were all tied in a barnyard.

Throwing open the gate I ordered a counter-charge, to which my men promptly responded. The Yankees never dreaming of our assuming the offensive, terrified at the yells of the men as they dashed on, they broke and fled in every direction. We drove them in confusion seven or eight miles down the pike. We left on the field nine of them killed — among them a captain and lieutenant — and about fifteen too badly wounded for removal; in this lot two lieutenants. We brought off 82 prisoners, many of these also wounded. I have since visited the scene of the fight. The enemy sent up a flag of truce for their dead and wounded, but many of them being severely wounded, they established a hospital on the ground. The surgeon who attended them informs me that a great number of those who escaped were wounded. The force of the enemy was six companies of the First Vermont Cavalry, one of their oldest and best regiments, and the prisoners inform me that they had every available man with them. There were certainly not less than 200; the prisoners say it was more than that. I had about 65 men in this affair. In addition to the prisoners, we took all their arms and about 100 horses and equipments. Privates Hart, Hurst, Keyes and Davis were wounded. The latter has since died. Both on this and several other occasions they have borne themselves with conspicuous gallantry. In addition to those mentioned above I desire to place on record the names of several others, whose promptitude and boldness in closing in with the enemy contributed much to the success of the fight. They are Lieutenant Chapman (late of Dixie Artillery), Sergt. Hunter and Privates Wellington and Harry Hatcher, Turner, Wild, Sowers, Ames and Sibert. There are many others, I have no doubt, deserving of honorable mention, but the above are only those who came under my personal observation. I confess that on this occasion I had not taken sufficient precautions to guard against surprise. It was 10 [o'clock] at night when I reached the place where the fight came off on the succeeding day. We had ridden through snow and mud upwards of 40 miles, and both men and horses were nearly broken down; besides, the enemy had fallen back a distance of about 18 miles. . . .

JOHN S. MOSBY,
Captain Commanding.

Maj.-Gen. J. E. B. Stuart.

[*Indorsements.*]

Headquarters Cavalry Division,
April 11, 1863.

Respectfully forwarded, as in perfect keeping with his other brilliant achievements. Recommended for promotion.

J. E. B. STUART,
Major-General.

HEADQUARTERS ARMY NORTHERN VIRGINIA,
April 13, 1863.

Respectfully forwarded for the information of the Department.   Telegraphic reports already sent in.

R. E. LEE, *General.*

APRIL 22, 1863.

ADJUTANT-GENERAL : — Nominate as major if it has not been previously done.

J. A. S. [SEDDON], *Secretary.*

CHAPTER VIII.

" Olympicum pulverem collegisse juvat." — *Horace.*

AFTER the fight at Chantilly and division of the booty the men who were with me, as usual, disappeared. Of the original fifteen who had come with me from the army for temporary service, five or six had been captured one night at a dancing frolic. Beattie was not in this party when he was made a prisoner, but was captured in a fight. I gave notice of a meeting at Rector's X roads, in Loudoun County, for the 31st of March. I had no idea until I got on the ground how many men I would have to go with me on my next raid, although I was confident that the success of my last one would attract a good many soldiers who were then at their homes on furlough. I was promptly there at the appointed time, and very soon sixty-nine men mustered to go with me. This was the largest force I had ever commanded up to that time. The shaking up of a kaleidoscope does not produce more variegated colors that the number of strange faces that appeared among them. I had never seen more than a dozen of them before, and very few of them had ever seen each other. I remember that there were several of the Black Horse Company with them. The force, therefore, lacked the cohesion and esprit de corps which springs from discipline and the mutual confidence of men who have long been associated together. I had no subordinate officer to aid me in command. They were better dressed, but almost as motley a crowd as Falstaff's regiment. There were representatives of nearly all the cavalry regiments in the army, with a sprinkling of men from the infantry, who had determined to try their luck on horseback. A good many of this latter class had been disabled for performing infantry duty by wounds ; there were others who had been absent from their regiments without leave ever since the first battle of Bull Run. There were a number of the wounded men who carried their crutches along tied to their saddle bows. As soon as their commanders heard that I had reclaimed and converted them once more into good soldiers they not only made requisition to have them returned to their regiments, but actually complained to General Lee of their being with me.

Now I took a practical and not a technical view of the question, and when a man volunteered to go into a fight with me 1 did not consider it to be any more a duty of mine to investigate his military record than his pedigree. Although a revolutionary government, none was ever so much under the domination of red tape as the one at Richmond. The martinets who controlled it were a good deal like the hero of Moliere's comedy, who complained that his antagonist had wounded him by thrusting in *carte*, when, according to the rule, it should have been in *tierce*. I cared nothing for the form of a thrust if it brought blood. I did not play with foils. The person selected to feed the army was a metaphysical dyspeptic, who it is said, lived on rice-water, and had a theory that soldiers could do the same. A man, to fill such a position well, should be in sympathy with hungry men, on the principle that he who drives fat oxen must himself be fat. When I received these complaints, which were sent through, but did not emanate from headquarters, I notified the men that they were forbidden any longer to assist me in destroying the enemy. They would sorrowfully return to their homes. It was no part of my contract to spend my time in the ignoble duty of catching deserters. I left that to those whose taste was gratified in doing the work. Several of these men, who had been very efficient with me, were, on my application, transferred to me by the Secretary of War. I always had a Confederate fire in my rear as well as that of the public enemy in my front. I will add that I never appealed in vain for justice either to General R. E. Lee, General Stuart, or the Secretary of War, Mr. Seddon.

And now, again, on the 31st of March, I set out once more to tempt fortune in the Fairfax forests. The men who followed me with so much zeal were not, perhaps, altogether of the saintly character or excited by the pious aspirations of the Canterbury pilgrims who knelt at the shrine of Thomas à Becket. Patriotism, as well as love of adventure, impelled them. If they got rewards in the shape of horses and arms, these were devoted, like their lives, to the cause in which they were fighting. They were made no richer by what they got, except in the ability to serve their country. I did not hope for much on this expedition. The enemy had grown wary and were prepared for attack at every point. But I knew that if I dispersed the men without trying to do something I would never see them again.

The spring campaign was about to open, and most of them would soon be recalled to the army, and I would be left a major without a command. I concluded to attack the detached cavalry camp at Dranesville. In a letter to Stuart a few weeks before, I had suggested that the cavalry brigade then stationed at Culpepper Court House should do this. I said: "There are about three hundred cavalry at Dranesville who are isolated from the rest of the command, so that nothing would be easier than to capture the whole force. I have harassed them so much that they do not keep their pickets over half a mile from camp." For some reason, Stuart did not undertake it. The reason was, I suppose, that he was saving his cavalry for the hard work they would have to do as soon as Hooker crossed the Rappahannock.

The enterprise looked hazardous, but I calculated on being able to surprise the camp, and trusted a good deal to my usual good luck. Ames, Dick Moran, Major Hibbs, and John Underwood, who never failed to be on time, went with me. I thought I would vary my tactics a little this time, and attack about dusk. They would hardly look for me at vespers; heretofore I had always appeared either in the daytime or late at night. I got to Herndon Station, where I had had the encounter two weeks before with the Vermont cavalry, about sundown, and learned there that the camp at Dranesville, which was about three miles off, had been broken up on the day before, and the cavalry had been withdrawn beyond Difficult Run, several miles below. This stream has its proper name, as there are few places where it can be crossed, and I knew that these would be strongly guarded. So it was hopeless to attempt anything in that direction. As I was so near, I concluded to go on to Dranesville that night, in hopes that by chance I might pick up some game. After spending an hour or so there, we started up the Leesburg pike to find a good place with forage for camping that night. I expected that our presence would be reported to the cavalry camps below, which would probably draw out a force which I could venture to meet. As all the forage had been consumed for several miles around, we had to march five or six miles to find any. About midnight we stopped at Miskel's farm, which is about a mile from the turnpike and just in the forks of Goose Creek and the Potomac.

Although it was the last day of March, snow was still lying on the ground, and winter lingered on the banks of the Potomac. My authority over the men was of such a transitory nature that I disliked to order them to do anything but fight. Hence I did not put out any pickets on the pike. The men had been marching all day, and were cold and tired. The enemy's camps were about fifteen miles below, and I did not think they could possibly hear of us before the next morning, when we would be ready for them, if they came after us. We fed and picketed our horses inside the barnyard, which was surrounded by a strong fence. Sentinels were stationed as a guard over the horses, and to arouse us in the event of alarm. Many of the men went to bed in the hay-loft, while others, including myself, lay down on the floor in the front room of the dwelling-house, before a big log fire. With my head on my saddle as a pillow, I was soon in a deep sleep. We were within a few hundred yards of the river, and there were Union camps on the other side; but I had no fear of them that night. About sunrise the next morning, I had just risen and put on my boots when one of the men came in and said that the enemy on the hill over the river was making signals. I immediately went out into the back yard to look at them. I had hardly done so, when I saw Dick Moran coming at full speed across the field, waving his hat, and calling out, "The Yankees are coming!"

He had stopped about two miles below, near the pike, and spent the night with a friend; and just as he woke up, about daylight, he had seen the column of Union cavalry going up the pike on our trail. By taking a short cut across the fields, he managed to get to us ahead of them. The barnyard was not a hundred yards from the house; and we all rushed to it. But not more than one-third of our horses were then bridled and saddled. I had buckled on my arms as I came out of the house. By the time we got to the inclosure where our horses were, I saw the enemy coming through a gate just on the edge of a clump of woods about two hundred yards off. The first thing I said to the men was that they must fight. The enemy was upon us so quick that I had no time to bridle or saddle my horse, as I was busy giving orders. I directed the men not to fire, but to saddle and mount quickly. The Union cavalry were so sure of their prey that they shut the gates after passing through, in order to prevent any of us from escaping. As Capt. Flint dashed forward at the head of his squadron, their sabres flashing in the rays of the morning sun, I felt like my final hour had come. Another squadron, after getting into the open field, was at the same time moving around to our rear. In every sense, things looked rather blue for us. We were in the angle of two impassable streams and surrounded by at least four times our number, with more than half of my men unprepared for a fight. But I did not despair. I had great faith in the efficacy of a charge; and in the affair at Chantilly had learned the superiority of the revolver over the sabre. I was confident that we could at least cut our way through them. The Potomac resounded with the cheers of the troops on the northern bank, who were anxious spectators, but could not participate in the conflict. When I saw Capt. Flint divide his command, I knew that my chances had improved at least fifty per cent. When he got to within fifty yards of the gate of the barnyard, I opened the gate and advanced, pistol in hand, on foot to meet him, and at the same time called to the men that had already got mounted to follow me. They responded with one of those demoniac yells which those who once heard never forgot, and dashed forward to the conflict " as reapers descend to the harvest of death." Just as I passed through the gate, at the head of the men, one of them, Harry Hatcher, the bravest of the brave, seeing me on foot, dismounted, and gave me his horse. Our assailants were confounded by the tactics adopted, and were now in turn as much surprised as we had been. They had thought that we would remain on the defensive, and were not prepared to receive an attack. I mounted Harry Hatcher's horse, and led the charge. In a few seconds Harry was mounted on a captured one whose rider had been killed. When the enemy saw us coming to meet them they halted, and were lost.

The powerful moral effect of our assuming the offensive, when nothing but surrender had been expected, seemed to bewilder them. Before they could recover from the shock of their surprise Captain Flint, the leader, had fallen dead in their sight. Be-

fore the impetuous onset of my men they now broke
and fled. No time was given them to re-form and
rally. The remorseless revolver was doing its work
of death in their ranks, while their swords were as
harmless as the wooden sword of harlequin. Unlike
my adversaries, I was trammelled with no tradition
that required me to use an obsolete weapon. The
combat was short, sharp and decisive. In the first
moment of collision, they wheeled and made for the
gate which they had already closed against themselves.
The other squadron that had gone around us, when
they saw their companions turn and fly, were panic-
stricken and forgot what they had been sent to do.
Their thoughts were now how to save themselves.
Our capture was now out of the question. They
now started pell-mell for the gate in order to reach
it ahead of us. But by this time our men had all
mounted, and like so many furies were riding and
shooting among their scattered ranks. The gate was
at last broken through by the pressure, but they
became so packed and jammed in the narrow passage
that they could only offer a feeble resistance, and at
this point many fell under the deadly fire that was
poured in from behind. Everywhere above the storm
of battle could be heard the voices and seen the
forms of the Dioscuri — "Major" Hibbs and Dick
Moran — cheering on the men as they rode headlong

in the fight. Dick Moran got into a hand-to-hand conflict in the woods with a party, and the issue was doubtful, when Harry Hatcher came up and decided it. There was with me that day a young artillery officer — Samuel F. Chapman — who at the first call of his State to arms had quit the study of divinity and become, like Stonewall Jackson, a sort of military Calvin, singing the psalms of David as he marched into battle. I must confess that his character as a soldier was more on the model of the Hebrew prophets than the Evangelist or the Baptist in whom he was so devout a believer. Before he got to the gate Sam had already exhausted every barrel of his two pistols and drawn his sabre. As the fiery Covenanter rode on his predestined course the enemy's ranks withered wherever he went. He was just in front of me — he was generally in front of everybody in a fight — at the gate. It was no fault of the Union cavalry that they did not get through faster than they did, but Sam seemed to think that it was. Even at that supreme moment in my life, when I had just stood on the brink of ruin and had barely escaped, I could not restrain a propensity to laugh.

Sam, to give more vigor to his blows, was standing straight up in his stirrups, dealing them right and left with all the theological fervor of Burly of Balfour. I doubt whether he prayed that day for

the souls of those he sent over the Stygian river.
I made him a captain for it. The chase was kept
up for several miles down the pike. When the people at Dranesville saw Capt. Flint pass through that
morning in search of me, they expected to see him
return soon with all of us prisoners. Among the
first fugitives who had passed through, and showed
the day's disasters in his face, was a citizen who
had hurried down the night before to the camp of
the Vermont cavalry to tell them where I was.
Thinking that Captain Flint had an easy thing of
it, he had ridden with him as a pilot, to witness
my humiliation and surrender. He escaped capture,
but never returned to his home during the war. I
doubt whether his loyalty ever received any reward.
He was also the first man to get back to the camp
he had left that morning on Difficult Run, where
he was about as welcome as the messenger who
bore to Rome the tidings of Cannæ. The reverend
Sam was not satisfied with the amount of execution
he had done at the gate, but continued his slaugh-
ter until, getting separated in the woods from the
other men, he dashed into a squad of the Vermont
men, who were doing their best to get away, and
received a cut with a sabre. But one of my men,
Hunter, came to his rescue, and the matter in dis-
pute was quickly settled. Down the pike the Ver-

mont cavalry sped, with my men close at their heels. Lieutenant Woodbury had got three miles away, when a shot from Ames laid him low. They never drew rein or looked back to see how many were behind them. I got pretty close to one, who, seeing that he was bound to be shot or caught, jumped off his horse and sat down on the roadside. As I passed him he called out to me, "You have played us a nice April fool, boys!" This reminded me that it was the first day of April. Some of the men kept up the pursuit beyond Dranesville, but I stopped there. The dead and wounded were strewn from where the fight began, at Miskel's, for several miles along the road. I had one man killed and three slightly wounded. I knew that as soon as the news reached the camps in Fairfax a heavy force would be sent against me, so I started off immediately, carrying eighty-three prisoners and ninety-five horses, with all their equipments.

At Dranesville were two sutlers' stores that had not been removed by their owners when the camps were broken up. These were, of course, appropriated, and helped to swell the joy of the partisans. A more hilarious party never went to war or a wedding than my men were returning home. Danger always gives a keener relish for the joys of life. They struck up a favorite song of Tom Moore's,

" The wine cup is sparkling before us," and the woods resounded with the melody. The dead and wounded were left on the field to be cared for by citizens until their friends could come after them. The number of prisoners I took exceeded the number of my men. One of my command — Frank Williams — had ridden early that morning to the house of a farmer to get his breakfast. The Vermont cavalry came up and got between him and us, and so Frank had to retreat. He, however, took two of them prisoners who had straggled off on the same errand, and carried them along with him. As he had seen such an overwhelming force go down upon us, and as he knew that we were hemmed in by deep water on two sides, Frank took it for granted that my star had set forever. He started off to carry the news, and reached Middleburg that day, when he informed the citizen of what he supposed was our fate. There was, of course, loud lamentation over it, for many had a son or a brother or a lover there. Frank had been there an hour or so anxiously waiting to hear something from us, but dreading the worst, when suddenly a blue column was seen coming up the pike. As blue was the predominant color, the first impression was that the men in gray were prisoners. But soon Dick Moran, who was riding in front, solved all doubts and fears as, with a voice louder than a Triton's shell, he proclaimed, "All right."

HEADQUARTERS, CAMP FRED'S, April 4, 1863.

MR. PRESIDENT : — Maj. John S. Mosby reports that he was attacked early on the morning of the 2d [1st] instant, near Dranesville, by about 200 Vermont cavalry. He promptly repulsed them, leaving on the field 25 killed and wounded, including 3 officers, and brought off 82 prisoners, with their horses, arms, and equipments. His force consisted of 65 men, and his loss was 4 wounded.

The enemy has evacuated Dranesville.

I had the pleasure to send by return courier to Major Mosby his commission of major of Partisan Rangers, for which I am obliged to your Excellency.

I am, with great respect, your obedient servant,

R. E. LEE,
General.

HIS EXCELLENCY JEFFERSON DAVIS,
President Confederate States of America, Richmond, Va.

———

HEADQUARTERS, STAHEL'S CAVALRY DIVISION,
FAIRFAX COURT HOUSE, VA.,
April 2, 1863.

GENERAL : — I have the honor to submit the following report, which is, however, made up from verbal information received from Col. Price, Lieutenant-Colonel Johnstone, and Major Taggart. I will forward the written report as soon as it is received, and shall take all possible means to ascertain the true state of the case. It appears that on the evening of the 31st ultimo, Major Taggart, at Union Church, 2 miles above Peach Grove, received information that Mosby, with about 65 men, was near Dranesville. He

immediately despatched Captain Flint, with 150 men of the
First Vermont, to rout or capture Mosby and his force. Captain Flint followed the Leesburg and Alexandria road to the
road which branches off to the right, just this side of Broad
Run. Turning to the right, they followed up the Broad
Run toward the Potomac, to a place marked "J. Mesed"
[Miskel]. Here, at a house, they came on to Mosby, who
was completely surprised and wholly unprepared for an attack from our forces. Had a proper disposition been made
of our troops, Mosby could not, by any possible means,
have escaped. It seems that around this house was a high
board fence and a stone wall, between which and the road
was also another fence and ordinary farm gate. Captain
Flint took his men through the gate, and, at a distance from
the house, fired a volley at Mosby and his men, who were
assembled about the house, doing but slight damage to
them. He then ordered a sabre charge, which was also
ineffectual, on account of the fence which intervened.
Mosby waited until the men were checked by the fence,
and then opened his fire upon them, killing and wounding
several. The men here became panic-stricken, and fled
precipitately toward this gate, through which to make their
escape. The opening was small, and they got wedged
together, and a fearful state of confusion followed ; while
Mosby's men followed them up, and poured into the crowd
a severe fire. Here, while endeavoring to rally his men,
Captain Flint was killed, and Lieutenant Grout, of the same
company, mortally wounded (will probably die to-day).
Mosby's men followed in pursuit, and sabred several of
our men on the road. Mosby, during his pursuit, is supposed to have received a sabre wound across the face which

unhorsed him. The rebels took some prisoners, and a number of horses, and fell back in great haste. In comparison to the number engaged, our loss was very heavy. As soon as Major Taggart received the report, he sent Major Hall in pursuit of Mosby, and to bring in our killed and wounded. Upon receiving the first intelligence, I immediately sent out Colonel Price with a detachment of the Sixth and Seventh Michigan and First Virginia [Union] Cavalry, who searched in every direction ; but no trace could be found of Mosby or his men, as information reached me too late.

I regret to be obliged to inform the commanding general that the forces sent out by Major Taggart missed so good an opportunity of capturing this rebel guerilla. It is only to be ascribed to the bad management on the part of the officers and the cowardice of the men. I have ordered Colonel Price to make a thorough investigation of this matter, and shall recommend those officers who are guilty to be stricken from the rolls.

The list of killed and wounded will be forwarded as soon as received.

I have the honor to remain, your obedient servant,

JUL. STAHEL,

Major-General.

MAJ. GEN. S. P. HEINTZELMAN,

Commanding, &c.

CHAPTER IX.

" And thou, Dalhousie, thou great god of war,
Lieutenant-Colonel to the Earl of Mar." — *Waller.*

WHAT in the newspaper slang of the day were termed "the depredations of guerillas," in the vicinity of Washington, induced the authorities there to make a change in outpost commanders. Wyndham, having played an unsuccessful game for over two months, during which time his headquarters had been raided, and his coat and hat carried off by us in his absence, had given it up in despair, and been sent to join his regiment at the front. The new person selected for the position was a major-general in the army, and a whiskered pandour, whose experience in foreign wars, it was hoped, would devise a remedy to suppress these annoyances. As soon as he took command, the cavalry camps in Fairfax resounded with the busy notes of preparation for a grand expedition, which he had resolved to undertake against us. It could no longer be endured that the war should be waged in full view of the dome of the Capitol, and the outposts could not stand the wear and tear of a perpetual skirmish, and the worry of lying awake all night waiting for an invisible foe to come and kill or capture them.

The spring campaign was about to open, and if the hostile band that created this trouble could be exterminated, the cavalry division, then doing duty in Fairfax, might be thrown forward to the Rappahannock to aid Hooker's operations. The Major-General was firmly persuaded, as no one had ever seen our camp, that the so-called guerillas were nobody but the country farmers, who collected together at night to make their incursions, and dispersed by day to take care of their fields and flocks. The fights at Chantilly and Dranesville ought to have convinced him that the men who had routed his best regiments had some training in war, and were no such irregular band as he imagined. It is true that, after I began operations in that region, many took up arms and joined me, who up to that time had followed peaceful pursuits. But whenever a citizen joined me and became a soldier, he discarded the habiliments of peace, put on his arms and uniform, and laid aside every other occupation.

When the struggle was over, they relapsed into the habits of their former life, and like the Puritan soldiers of Cromwell, became as marked for devotion to their civil duties as they had ever been in war. As for myself, it was for a long time maintained that I was a pure myth, and my personal identity was as stoutly denied as that of Homer or the Devil. All historic doubts about my own existence have, I believe, been settled; but the fables published by the Bohemians who followed the army made an impression that still lives in popular recollection.

There is a lingering belief that my command was not a part of the regularly organized military force of the Southern Confederacy. The theory of the Major-General, though contradicted by facts staring him in the face every day, got a lodgement in the minds of some people which has never been effaced. It was to confirm it that he now undertook to make a reconnoissance through the region infested by us. It happened that just at that time Hooker was preparing once more to cross the Rappahannock, and as a preliminary movement had sent Stoneman with the cavalry corps up the river to seize the Orange and Alexandria railroad and hold it as the line of communication with Washington. The line that connects an army with its base of supplies is the heel of Achilles — its most vital and vulnerable point. It is a great achievement in war to compel an enemy to make heavy detachments to guard it; it is equally as great a one to destroy the force that threatens it. It was to effect this latter object that in April, 1863, the Major-General set out on his expedition against me with two brigades of cavalry and a battery of artillery, which was to be the prelude of the opening of the campaign on the Rappahannock. Now it so happened that just about that time I received a letter from Stuart suggesting the capture of a train on the railroad. The effect of such a stroke of course would be to create uneasiness and alarm about the safety of Hooker's supplies.

The following is an extract from Stuart's letter: "There is now a splendid opportunity to strike the enemy in the rear of Warrenton Junction; the trains are running regularly to that point. Capture a train and interrupt the operation of the railroad, though it may be, by the time you get this, the opportunity may be gone. Stoneman's main body of cavalry is located near Warrenton Junction, Bealton and Warrenton Springs. Keep far enough away from a brigade camp to give you time to get off your plunder and prisoners. Information of the movements of large bodies is of the greatest importance to us just now. The marching or transportation of divisions will often indicate the plan of a campaign. Be sure to give dates and numbers and names, as far as possible."

I could offer no better proof than this letter of the useful services that may be rendered by an active partisan corps in co-operation with the movements of an army. It not only cripples an adversary, but communicates intelligence of his movements. Accordingly I gave notice for a meeting at Upperville to undertake an enterprise against the railroad. I was willing to let the Union troops down in Fairfax rest while I turned my attention to Joe Hooker. On the evening of the day before the meeting I had been with Beattie up to the mountain to get a fresh horse to ride on the raid, and we returned about dark. I met a citizen, who informed me that a large Federal force was camped at Middleburg, and that there had been artillery firing there during the afternoon. I thought it was merely a false report that had gotten up a stampede, for I had not heard the firing, and I could not conceive what they could have been firing at, as we had no troops about there. I supposed that if they had come after me they would have tried to keep it a secret and make as little noise as possible.

About nine o'clock that night Beattie and I rode down in the direction of Middleburg to find out if there was any truth in the rumor. When we got on a high hill, about a mile off, that overlooks the town, we stopped to reconnoitre. The night was very cold, with a drizzling rain. Not a single camp-fire could be seen anywhere; and there was nothing to indicate the bivouacs of a military force. I said to Beattie: "This is just as I said — nothing but a stampede about nothing. If there were any troops about there, they would have camp-fires on such a cold night as this." We then rode forward, but had only gone a few hundred yards farther when we were halted and fired on by a picket. This, of course, proved that the rumor was true.

We fell back. But it was a mystery I could not solve, why there should be an encampment of troops in such weather without fires. Then, too, there had been artillery firing; what could possibly have been the reason for that? The next morning I went, according to appointment, to meet my men at Upperville, having sent out some scouts toward Middleburg, which is eight miles distant. My desire was to let the Union cavalry alone at Middleburg and strike the meditated blow at Hooker, on the railroad. The force that had come up from Fairfax after me had now been practically eliminated from the campaign. I wanted, therefore, if possible, to slip away from them undiscovered. Early that morning the Major-General put his column in motion on the pike for Upperville; but he had only gone a couple of miles before his advance-guard was driven in by Tom Richards and a few men. This caused him to halt and get ready for action. On the day before, on his march up the turnpike, he had seen horsemen on the hills watching him, who, like the Arab when he folds his tent, had silently stolen away.

On reaching Middleburg, the clouds seemed to thicken around him; for he had seen at least a dozen perched on the heights at different places gazing at him. They were evidently ready to light down on any stragglers, and bear them off in their talons. The Major-General unlimbered his guns, and opened fire on every moving object in his sight. He did no damage to anybody; but his firing gave notice for miles around to people to get out of his way. There was a large grove near Middleburg, in which he proposed to bivouac that night. But before entering it, he shelled it so effectively as not only to expel any guerillas that might be lurking there, but all animated nature. He carried along a newspaper correspondent to chronicle his exploits. His letter, published in the New York *Tribune* shortly after that, made clear a number of things which I had not been able to understand before reading it. It praised his consummate skill and prudence in allowing no camp-fires during the night, as they would have lighted the way for the guerillas to attack him; while the destructive artillery fire with which he had raked the forest showed that he possessed the

foresight of a great general. It was also stated that
he would only permit one half of his command to
sleep at a time or unbridle and unsaddle their
horses. With unconscious irony the letter concluded
by stating that the result of the expedition had
demonstrated that Mosby hadn't over twenty-five
men, who had been totally exterminated. After
remaining in line of battle for some time, waiting
for me to attack him, the Major-General determined
not to advance any farther toward Upperville, which
lies just at the base of the Blue Ridge.

It was surmised that the guerillas, like the Cy-
clops, had taken refuge in caves on the mountain-
side, and there might be danger in approaching too
closely, so he turned squarely off to his left. On
his line of march he had swept the country of all
the old men he could find, for he was firmly persuaded that in doing so he was breaking up my
band. No plea in defence would be heard. A man
named Hutchison, who was 70 years old, and had
always used crutches, was among the prisoners. In
vain he pleaded his age and infirmities as proof of
the impossibility of his being a guerilla. A Vermont soldier stepped forward, and swore that he
saw him leading the charge in the fight at Miskel's
farm. He was sent to Washington as a trophy.
The captives under guard marched in the rear of
the column.

About eighty men had met me at Upperville. In order to elude thé Major-General, and execute my plan of capturing a train on the railroad, I made a detour by Salem, going on toward Thoroughfare Gap in the Bull Run Mountains. The Major-General and myself, being ignorant of each other's plans, had also gone the same way, in order to avoid meeting the force that had driven in his advance from Upperville. Somehow he had got the idea in his head that a large body of Stuart's cavalry was in the neighborhood, and he was not looking for them. An hour or so after I had passed through Salem, the Major-General arrived there. He had started to return to Fairfax by making a circuit around through Thoroughfare Gap. Without any design on his part, he had struck right on my track. As I was marching very leisurely, — for I did not want to get to the railroad until about dark, — he might easily have overtaken me; but he did not seem to have the least desire to do so. He followed me at the rate of half a mile an hour. Having got all the old farmers prisoners, the measure of his ambition was full. He had at last destroyed the nest of vipers. He did not believe the body of cavalry that had gone on ahead were the very men he pretended to be looking for.

Just as I reached Thoroughfare Gap, two of my

men — Alfred Glasscock and Norman Smith — came galloping up, and said that the enemy was pursuing me. They had, for some reason, remained behind at Salem, and saw the Major-General's command march through along the same road I was on. As he was only one hour behind me there, I felt certain that he was almost upon me. Some four miles back of where I was, the roads forked at a village called the Plains, one leading to Thoroughfare, and the other to Hopewell Gap in the Bull Run Mountains. I immediately wheeled around, and crossed over on the Hopewell road and started back toward the Plains. I supposed the Major-General was in pursuit of me, and as I could not undertake with less than 100 men to attack in front 4000 cavalry and a battery of artillery, my intention was to try to cut off his rear-guard before it passed the forks or the gap. But when I got on a high hill overlooking the Plains, instead of meeting his rear-guard, when I rode forward to reconnoitre, I saw his advance, that had just got to the forks. I halted, so did they, while their whole column rapidly deployed in line of battle, and the guns were placed in battery, ready for the expected onset.

Every disposition was made by him to receive an attack. We stayed there facing each other over one hour, until it grew dark, when I disbanded my men.

I had abandoned my enterprise against the railroad because I supposed that it had been discovered where I was going, and that if I went on, with the Major-General behind me and Stoneman's cavalry in front, we would all be captured. He had learned at Salem that a body of cavalry had passed through just ahead of him, and at the Plains he saw that they had gone on the Thoroughfare road.

After giving us, as he supposed, ample time to get away, he started on the same route, when, with surprise, he saw a body of cavalry threatening him on the Hopewell road. He had no idea they were the same cavalry whose track he was on. If he continued his line of march he must go through one of the mountain passes, and remembering the fate of the Persians at Thermopylæ, he determined now to halt. I took it for granted that he had stopped to go into camp at the Plains. But he, not knowing that I had disbanded my command and fearing a night attack, as soon as it became dark began a retreat back toward Middleburg. Being a cautious general, he did not go along the main public road, but cut across fields and took private ways. The bridges across every stream he crossed were broken down after he passed, although some were so narrow that a man could jump over them, and trees were felled across the road to prevent us from charging his rear. After marching all night he reached the vicinity of Middleburg about daybreak and went into camp. He had no idea that I had disbanded my men and gone off, but thought he had eluded us. Now, it had never entered my head that he was going to run away from me. Beattie and I had ridden on the same night over near Middleburg, and I stopped at the house of George McArty. About daybreak he came running to where we were sleeping and called out to us : "Boys! get up quick — the Yankees are all around you." We jumped up, and two or three hundred yards away we could see the field was blue with the Major-General's command. We bridled and saddled our horses quickly and rode off unmolested in full view of them. The Major-General and I had been running away from each other a whole day and night, and then came very near sleeping together. After taking a short rest from the fatigue of his night march, he started back to Fairfax with the battalion of graybeards he had taken prisoners, riding bareback with blind bridles on broken-down plow-horses. They were marched down to Washington and paraded through the streets to gratify the curiosity of the people. They created a greater sensation than a circus. Such was the grand anti-climax to the Major-General's Anabasis. It is so unique and complete in itself that I will not mar its epic unity by adding anything more to the narrative.

Capt. Mosby, with his command, entered this town this morning at 2 A.M. They captured my patrols, horses, &c. They took Brigadier-General Stoughton and horses, and all his men detached from his brigade. They took every horse that could be found, public and private ; and the commanding officer of the post, Colonel Johnstone, of the Fifth New York Cavalry, made his escape from them in a nude state by accident. They searched for me in every direction, but being on the Vienna road visiting outposts, I made my escape.   L. L. CONNOR, *Provost-Marshal.*

P. S. All our available cavalry forces are in pursuit of them.   MAJ. HUNT, *Asst. Adjt. Gen.*

GENERAL HEINTZELMAN'S HEADQUARTERS.

Genl. Stahel's report to War Dept. says : "On the 13th day of March, 1863, the day after General Stoughton was captured at Fairfax C. H., I was on my way from Stafford Court House to New York, on eight days' leave of absence. Upon my arrival in Washington, I was summoned to report at once to President Lincoln. He told me of the capture of Genl. Stoughton and the insecure condition of our lines in front of Washington. The President also said that he desired to have me in command in front of Washington to put a stop to these raids. He wrote a letter to Gen. Heintzelman, comdg. the Dept. of Washington, and directed me to go and see him. . . . On the same day, the 17th of March, I was appointed Major-General of Volunteers, to take date from the 14th of March, 1863."

Gen. Stahel was relieved of his cavalry command on June 28th, 1863.

HEQRS. STAHEL'S CAV. DIV., DEPT. OF WASHINGTON,
FAIRFAX COURT HOUSE, April 11, 1863.

GENERAL : — I have the honor to report with regard to
the reconnoissance under command of Brig.-Gen. J. F.
Copeland, which left this place on the 3d day of April,
and returned here early on the morning of the 6th instant,
that it proceeded as far as Middleburg, and searched dili-
gently through that whole section of country without meeting any enemy in force or ascertaining definitely the whereabouts of Mosby.   Small detachments of rebels, however,
were occasionally seen, but scattered on the approach of
our troops.

On the 4th instant, early in the morning, in front of
Middleburg, a collision occurred between one of his pickets
and some of the enemy's, resulting in the death of one and
the wounding of another on each side.   During the expedition there were captured and arrested sixty-one prisoners,
citizens and soldiers, fifty-three horses, two mules, a quantity
of wheat, three wagons, saddles, bridles, guns, sabres, &c.,
all of which were turned over to the provost-marshal of
this place, and by him to Colonel Baker Washington, a copy
of whose receipt is inclosed within. . . . &c.

JUL. STAHEL,
Major-General.

MAJ.-GEN. S. P. HEINTZELMAN,
Commanding, &c.

There is no report on file of Major-General Stahel's expedition about two weeks after this in search of Mosby.

CHAPTER X.

" Our acts our angels are — or good **or ill,**
Our fatal shadows that walk by us still."

IF I had known at the time of the major-general's
expedition to Fauquier all that I know now, I
would not, of course, have abandoned the enterprise
against the railroad. I had thought that after he
struck my track at Salem, he was really in pursuit
of me, although he only followed at a terrapin's
pace. I could not have anticipated that a major-
general, starting out to win his spurs, would retreat
as soon as he got in sight of the object he was in
search of. I had disbanded my men, with instructions to meet me again in a few days at a certain
place. I wanted to give the major-general time to
get home, while I could recruit my forces, pick my
flint, and try again. As the troops that belonged
to the defences of Washington were now on the
defensive, it was my policy to let them alone, and
turn my attention to Hooker's army, which was then
preparing to cross the Rappahannock. I could most
efficiently aid Gen. Lee by assailing Hooker in the

rear. A partisan commander who acts in co-operation with an army should always, if possible, operate against troops engaged in offensive movements.
The Major-General was now resting on his laurels.
For two months preceding his raid into Fauquier,
there had been incessant attacks on the outposts,
and daily alarm through the camps. All this had
now suddenly ceased, and the quiet that reigned was
supposed to confirm the truth of the report of the
annihilation of my band.

On May 2, 70 or 80 men assembled at my call.
I had information that Stoneman's cavalry had left
Warrenton and gone south, which indicated that
the campaign had opened. My plan now was to
strike Hooker. The moral effect of a blow from
behind might have an important influence on the
result. I started for Warrenton, and reached there
about dusk, and learned that Stoneman was over
the river. It was not known whether or not the
Orange & Alexandria railroad was still held by the
Union troops. I went into camp near the town that
night, and started by daylight the next morning on
the road leading to Fredericksburg, which crosses
the railroad. I was sure that Hooker would not
repeat the blunder of Burnside, but would cross
at some of the upper fords of the Rappahannock.
It was toward one of these that my course was

directed. The roar of the guns at Chancellorsville could be distinctly heard, and we knew that the two armies were once more in the deadly embrace of battle.

It was not more than fifteen or twenty miles off ; and we could easily reach there early in the day. I wanted to contribute my mite of support to the Southern cause. When we were within a couple of miles of the railroad a bugle was heard ; and I turned aside and marched to the sound. I thought it must come from a cavalry camp, which we might sweep through as we went along. Before we had gone very far, an infantry soldier was caught, who informed me that I was marching right into the camp of an infantry brigade. I found out that there was some cavalry on the railroad at another point, and so I made for that. These troops had just been sent up to replace Stoneman's. I committed a great error in allowing myself to be diverted by their presence from the purpose of my expedition. They were perfectly harmless where they were, and could not help Hooker in the great battle then raging. I should, at least, have endeavored to avoid a fight by marching around them. If I had succeeded in destroying them all, it would hardly have been the equivalent of the damage I might have done to Hooker by appearing at United States ford during the agony

of the fight. There all of his wagons were packed.
It would be difficult to calculate the demoralizing
effect of the news on his army that the enemy was
in their rear, and their trains and rations were
burning up.

Just as we debouched from the woods in sight of
Warrenton Junction, I saw, about 300 yards in front
of us, a body of cavalry in the open field. It was a
bright, warm morning; and the men were lounging
on the grass, while their horses, with nothing but
their halters on, had been turned loose to graze on
the young clover. They were enjoying the music of
the great battle, and had no dream that danger was
near. Not a single patrol or picket had been put
out. At first they mistook us for their own men,
and had no suspicion as to who we were until I
ordered a charge and the men raised a yell. The
shouting and firing stampeded the horses, and they
scattered over a field of several hundred acres, while
their riders took shelter in some houses near by.
We very soon got all out of two houses; but the
main body took refuge in a large frame building
just by the railroad. I did not take time to dis-
mount my men, but ordered a charge on the house;
I did not want to give them time to recover from
their panic. I came up just in front of two windows
by the chimney, from which a hot fire was poured

that brought down several men by my side. But I paid them back with interest when I got to the window, into which I emptied two Colt's revolvers. The house was as densely packed as a sardine box; and it was almost impossible to fire into it without hitting somebody. The doors had been shut from the inside; but the Rev. Sam Chapman dismounted, and burst through, followed by John Debutts, Mountjoy, and Harry Sweeting. The soldiers in the lower rooms immediately surrendered; but those above held out. There was a haystack near by; and I ordered some of the hay to be brought into the house and fire to be set to it. Not being willing to be burned alive as martyrs to the Union, the men above now held out a white flag from a window. The house was densely filled with smoke and the floor covered with the blood of the wounded. The commanding officer, Maj. Steel, had received a mortal wound; and there were many others in the same condition. All who were able now came out of the house.

After a severe fight, I had taken three times my own number prisoners, together with all their horses, arms and equipments. Most of my men then dispersed over the field in pursuit of the frightened horses which had run away. I was sitting on my horse near the house, giving directions for getting ready to leave with the prisoners and spoil, when one of my men, named Wild, who had chased a horse some distance down the railroad, came at full speed, and reported a heavy column of cavalry coming up. I turned to one of my men, Alfred Glasscock, and said to him, "*Now we will whip them.*" I had hardly spoken the words when I saw a large body of Union cavalry, not over 200 or 300 yards off, rapidly advancing.

As I have stated, most of my command had scattered over the field, and the enemy was so close there was no time to rally and re-form before they got upon us. In attempting to do so, I remained on the ground until they were within 50 yards of me, and was nearly captured. So there was nothing to do but for every man to take care of himself. I have already described the kind of command I had at this time. They were a mere aggregation of men casually gathered, belonging to many different regiments, who happened to be in the country.[1] Of course, such a body has none of the cohesion and discipline that springs from organization, no matter how brave the men may be individually. Men never fought better than they did at the house, while the defenders were inspired to greater resistance, knowing that

---

[1] I had no subordinate officer to help me in command.

relief was near. We had defeated and captured three times our own number, and now had to give up the fruits of victory, and in turn to fly to prevent capture. My men fled in every direction, taking off about 50 horses and a number of prisoners. Only one of my men — Templeman — was killed, but I lost about 20 captured, nearly all of whom were wounded. Dick Moran was among them. I never made a better fight than this, although finally compelled to retreat before 10 times my own number.

As to its ulterior effects, it was about the same, as I shall hereafter show, as if I had not lost what I had won. The cavalry I had met was Deforest's brigade, that had come up the night before. As I have said, it was a mistake my making this fight, even if I had been completely successful. In all probability, it saved Hooker's transportation, just as the fight of the Prussians at the bridge of the Dyle saved Wellington, although they were beaten. It detained Grouchy long enough to keep him from Waterloo. I learned wisdom from experience, and after that always looked before I took a leap.

When I ordered the charge at Warrenton Junction, I had no idea whether I was attacking a hundred or a thousand men.

Just one year after that, I started with the purpose of attacking the rear of the army of the Potomac, at the same place where I had intended to strike Hooker. I found the railroad guarded, but I crossed it unnoticed in the dark, and went on. Lee and Grant had met in the Wilderness. Grant had all of his transportation south of the river, with cavalry pickets at the United States ford. There was no chance to get at it. Hooker had left his on the north bank where I was. I got one of Grant's trains near Aquia Creek, on the Lower Potomac; but when I returned, a few days after that, to get another, found that he had detached a cavalry force to protect that route. This was what I wanted to make him do. It was that number of men subtracted from his strength. After striking one blow at the line of supply of an army, a demonstration will generally answer all the purposes of an attack. Hooker did not stay in the Wilderness long enough for me to renew my attempt to get at his trains. When, after my rout, I appeared at Warrenton, attended by a single companion, where I had passed the night before with my command, I was apparently as forlorn as Charles,

> After dread Pultowa's day,
>   When fortune left the royal Swede.

But I felt no discouragement. My faith in my ability to create a command and continue my warfare on the border was still as unwavering as Francis

Xavier's when he left the Tagus, to plant the cross on the shores of Coromandel.

The enemy held the railroads as far south as the Rappahannock, and in a few days I got together 30 or 40 men, and started down again to strike them somewhere. I found the bridges over Broad Run and Kettle Run unguarded; we set fire to them and left them in a blaze. It had not been expected that we would come back so soon, hence their want of precaution to provide for their safety. While the bridges were burning, the soldiers who had been put there to protect them were dozing in their tents not a mile off. In a few days I again went as far as Dumfries, but could find no assailable point. The trains all carried strong infantry guards, in addition to those stationed along the railroad. I started back without having effected anything, and stopped at the house of a man named Lynn, to rest and feed our horses. As we were far inside the enemy's lines, there was some risk in this; but we were tired and hungry. Our horses had been unbitted, and were eating their corn, and I was lying on the grass asleep, when I was aroused by the cry that the enemy was coming. We barely had time to bridle up and mount before they were upon us. They came full speed on our trail, and were strung out for a long distance on the road. This was my

opportunity.   A lieutenant was gallantly leading
them.   I saved myself this time by the same coun-
ter-stroke that a few weeks before had rescued me
from the brink of ruin in the fight at Miskel's farm.
We did not wait for the danger, but went to meet it.
There was a gate across the road, between us and the
enemy, which I ordered to be opened.   We dashed
through, and in the moment of collision the lieutenant fell, severely wounded.   Several others in the
front met the same fate ; they had drawn sabres, that
hurt nobody, and we used pistols.   Their companions
halted, hesitated, and were overpowered before support could come up.   Some turned and fled, and in
doing so communicated their panic to those in their
rear.   They fled pell-mell back toward their camp,
leaving their dead and wounded on the field and a
number of prisoners and horses in our hands.   I
then had, in turn, to get away quickly.   I knew
they would soon return with reinforcements ; they
did come, but we were gone.

In returning, we crossed the railroad within a
mile of Manassas, and in full view of the troops
there, but were not molested.   I found out from
this raid the difficulty of making any impression
with my small command on the force guarding the
road.   I could keep them on the watch, and in a
state of anxiety and alarm ; but, while this might

satisfy Stuart and Gen. Lee, the men on whom I had to depend to do the work would not be content with such results. In order to retain them, it was necessary for me to stimulate their enthusiasm with something more tangible. War to them was not an abstraction ; it meant prisoners, arms, horses and sutler's stores ; remote consequences were not much considered. So I sent Beattie with a letter to explain the situation to Stuart, in which I said : "If you will let me have a mountain howitzer, I think I could use it with great effect, especially on the railroad trains. I have several experienced artillerists with me. The effect of such annoyance is to force the enemy to make heavy details to guard their communications. I have not attacked any of their railroad trains, because I have no ammunition for my carbines, and they are pretty strongly guarded with infantry." In this letter I suggested the theory on which my warfare was conducted. It would not only draw troops from the front, but prevent those doing duty on the railroad and around Washington from being sent to Hooker to make up his losses in the Wilderness. These operations were erratic simply in not being in accordance with the fixed rules taught by the academies ; but in all that I did there was a unity of purpose, and a plan which my commanding general understood and approved.

The Confederate drill sergeants could see no use in what they could not comprehend.

In reference to the fight at Warrenton Junction, Gen. Abercrombie reports:

"Between the hours of 9 and 10 A.M., on the morning of the 3d ult., an outpost of the 1st Va. [Union] Cavalry at Warrenton Junction, about 100 men, under Lieut.-Col. Krep's command, were surprised and attacked by Maj. Mosby, with his force of about 125 [75] men. The men of the 1st Va. were scattered about the station, their horses unsaddled, in order to be groomed and fed. Mosby's force came in upon them from the direction of Warrenton, which place they left at daylight. Their front rank was dressed in the uniform of the United States [we were all dressed in gray. J. S. M.], and they were supposed to be a force of Union cavalry until within a short distance, when they charged, and surrounded the house in and about which the 1st Va. lay. After a short fight, in which several of the rebels were killed and wounded, the men of the 1st Va. for the most part surrendered, and about 40 were being taken towards Warrenton by their captors, when a detachment of 70 men of the 5th N. Y. Cavalry, which was camped near by, under command of Maj. Hammond, came up, charged upon the rebels, and a running fight ensued, which was continued for five miles, in the course of which all the prisoners taken by Mosby were recaptured, with the exception of two."

Major-General Stahel reports:

"Our men being surprised and completely surrounded, rallied in a house close at hand, and where a sharp fight ensued. Our men defended themselves as long as their ammunition lasted, notwithstanding the Rebels built a large fire about the house, of hay and straw and brushwood; the flames reached the house, and their ammunition being entirely expended, they were obliged to surrender." Maj. Steele, of the 1st. Va., was mortally wounded in the house.

CHAPTER XI.

Quis jam fluctus, quae regio in terris non nostri plena laboris.
— *Æneid.*

AT this time Gen. Lee was making the preliminary movement of the Gettysburg campaign up
the left bank of the Rappahannock, while Hooker
moved on a parallel line on the other. Pleasanton's
cavalry corps was massed on the river, near Rappahannock station, about fifty miles from Washington,
which was now covered by Hooker's army. In compliance with my request, Stuart sent me a small
mountain howitzer by Beattie. A brigade of cavalry
and one of infantry were lying between Manassas
and Catlett's station; and here was the only possible
chance of reaching the railroad without being discovered. On May 29, 1863, I set out with about forty
men, and my little gun, to strike it somewhere between these points. I had no caisson; but carried
fifteen rounds of ammunition in the limber-chest.
The enterprise on which I was going, when judged
by the common standards of prudence, appeared not
only hazardous but foolhardy. The camps of the
enemy were distributed along the road at intervals of

one or two miles, with patrols continually passing. Every train had on board a strong infantry guard. If I should succeed in penetrating their lines and making a capture, it could not be done without alarming the camps, which would make my retreat difficult, if not impossible. But I thought the end justified the risk. An attack, even by my small band, at such a critical time, might create an important diversion in favor of Gen. Lee. If this could be done, then the loss of the gun, and even of my whole command, would be as dust in the balance against the advantage of it.

We bivouacked that night in the pines near Catlett's, and were awakened in the morning by the reveille in the Union camps, which were a mile or so distant on either side of us. There was a narrow pathway through the pines, along which we marched until within a hundred yards of the railroad. The telegraph wire was cut, and a rail sufficiently removed to allow a train to run off the track. The howitzer was in charge of the Rev. Sam Chapman, who had been so conspicuous in the fight at Miskel's; it was now made ready for action. All of us were under cover, with one man near the road to give notice of an approaching train. We had not waited long before he gave the signal. I rode forward, and saw it puffing along. Chapman rammed down a charge in his gun; and all awaited the event with breathless interest. I was in fear every moment of a patrol coming on the road who might give the alarm and stop the train. Fortunately, none came. The engineer, not suspecting danger, was driving at full speed, when suddenly the locomotive glided from the track. The infantry guard fired a volley, which did no injury to us except killing a horse. In an instant, a shell from Chapman's gun went crashing through the cars. They all jumped off and took to their heels through the pines. In the stampede, they did not take time to count our number. If they had stood their ground, they could have easily driven us away. Another shell was sent through the boiler of the engine. The infernal noise of the escaping steam increased the panic among the fugitives. There were several bales of hay on the train that were set on fire. The whole was soon in flames. One car was loaded with sutlers' goods, which the men did not permit to be entirely consumed by the fire. There was also a number of fresh shad; and each man secured one of these. The blockade of the Potomac had for a long time deprived us of that luxury. The United States mail bags were tied to the carriage of the howitzer; and we started to retrace our steps.

I have been criticised a good deal at the North for capturing trains on railroads used for military purposes. To justify myself, it is not necessary for me to use the *tu quoque* argument, and retort that my adversaries did the same whenever they could ; for the plain reason that I was simply exercising a belligerent right. There was nobody but soldiers on this train ; but, if there had been women and children, too, it would have been all the same to me. Those who travel on a road running through a military district must accept the risk of the accidents of war. It does not hurt people any more to be killed in a railroad wreck than having their heads knocked off by a cannon shot. One of the most effective ways of impeding the march of an army is by cutting off its supplies ; and this is just as legitimate as to attack it in line of battle. Jomini says that the irregular warfare of the Cossacks did more to destroy the French army on the expedition to Moscow than the élite regiments of the Russian guard. After the peace, all Europe hailed their hetman, Platoff, as the hero of the war, and the corporation of London gave him a sword.

But to return to my story. I had penetrated the enemy's lines, and the difficulty was now to get out. The sound of the cannon had given the alarm. The long roll was beaten through all the infantry camps, and the bugles sounded — "to horse." As I had never used a piece of artillery before, it was not known that I had it. It was thought at first that Stuart had come in behind them, and hence they advanced on me cautiously. When I had got about a mile from the railroad I met a regiment of New York cavalry (the 5th), in the road directly in front of me. It had come up from the camp below at Kettle Run to cut us off. We halted while Chapman unlimbered, and sent a shell at them, which, fortunately, burst at the head of the column, and killed the horse of the commanding officer. This created a stampede, and they scattered before another shell could get to them. The way was now open, and we went on by the horse lying with his accoutrements in the road. I made Foster and a few others gallop forward, to produce the impression that we were pursuing, but soon recalled them to the gun, as I was expecting the enemy every moment in my rear. We were now girt with foes on every side. It would, of course, have been easy to save ourselves by scattering through the woods, but I was fighting on a point of honor. I wanted to save the howitzer, or, if I had to lose it, I was determined to exact all that it was worth in blood. After we got about a mile further on, the regiment we had broken rallied, and with re-inforcements came on again in pursuit.

Another shell was thrown at them, and they fell back. We were just on the edge of a wood, and I ordered Chapman to go forward with his gun at a gallop, while I remained behind with six men as a rear-guard to cover the retreat.

Clouds of cavalry which had been attracted by the firing were now seen in different directions, and the enemy once more moved toward us. With less than 50 men I was confronting Deforest's brigade of cavalry. At one time we had been entirely enveloped by them, but had broken through their line. As the enemy came near we slowly withdrew. Their advance guard of 12 or 15 men suddenly dashed upon us as we were retiring through the woods. We wheeled and had a fierce hand-to-hand fight, in which they were routed and driven back. Several of their dead and wounded were left on the ground. I have before spoken of Capt. Hoskins, an English officer, who had recently joined me. He was riding by my side when the fight began. The tradition of chivalry inherited from the ancient knights of using the sword in single combat still asserted its dominion over him, but my other men had no more use for that antiquated weapon than a coat of mail. They had discarded it as a useless incumbrance. Hoskins was in the act of giving a thrust when he was shot. In an instant after, his adversary fell before a deadly revolver. Hoskins's wound was mortal. When the fight was over, he was taken to the house of an Englishman near by, and lived a day or two. Thus died as gallant a gentleman as ever pricked his steed over Palestine's plains. He had passed without a scar through the fire of the Redan and the Malakoff to fall in a petty skirmish in the American forests. I could not stay by him, and I had no means of carrying him off. The overwhelming numbers pressing upon us forced a retreat, and we had to leave him by the roadside with his life-blood ebbing fast away. The horse that I had presented to him disdained capture and followed us. I gave it to Beattie. He was buried in his martial cloak at Greenwich church, and now, like Lara,

> Sleeps not where his fathers sleep

Seeing that no hope was left us but to save our honor and stand by the gun, I sent Foster with an order to Chapman to halt and unlimber in a narrow lane on a hill. The high fences on both sides were some protection against a flank attack of cavalry. I knew we could hold the position as long as the ammunition lasted for the gun. Some of the men who had joined me, thinking that they were going on a picnic, had already left to fry their shad and eat the confectioneries they had got on the train. When

I rode up to Chapman, he had his gun already shotted. Mountjoy and Beattie were standing by it. Their faces beamed with what the Romans called the *gaudia certaminis*, and they had never looked so happy in their lives. As for myself, realizing the desperate straits we were in, I wished I was somewhere else.

Sam Chapman and his brother William, who afterward became the lieutenant-colonel of my battalion, had commanded the battery which, under Longstreet's orders, had shattered Fitz John Porter's corps in its assault on Jackson's line at Groveton heights. When the Federal cavalry came in sight a couple of hundred yards off, he sent them a shell that exploded in their ranks, and they fell back in confusion to the woods. They re-formed and came again. If they had deployed as foragers, we would have been driven away without inflicting much loss on them. But they committed the error of charging up the road in a solid column of fours, where every discharge from the gun raked them with grape and canister. They made several successive onsets of this kind, which Chapman repulsed. In turn, we would charge and drive them a considerable distance, and then return to the gun. This was repeated several times over ground strewn with their killed and wounded men and horses. The damage done here to my side was that Bill Elzey had several teeth knocked out by a bullet. They used their sabres, and we the revolver. At last the supreme moment came. Chapman had rammed home his last round of ammunition, and a heavy column was again advancing. I sat on my horse just behind the gun : when they got within 50 yards, it again belched with fire and knocked down a number of men and horses in their front. They halted, and, at the same time, I ordered a charge, and drove them down to the foot of the hill. I was riding a spirited sorrel horse, who carried me with so much force that I could not hold him up until I had gone some distance through their ranks. Charlie McDonough followed me. As I passed by a big cavalryman he struck me a blow with his sabre on the shoulder that nearly knocked me from my seat. At the same instant my pistol flashed, and he reeled from his saddle. McDonough and I were now hemmed in by high fences on both sides ; the Federal soldiers we had passed in the road, seeing that nearly all my men had left the gun, which had ceased firing, made a dash at it. Beattie managed to mount and get away. George Tuberville, who acted as driver, went off at full speed, and saved his two horses and limber-chest. Mountjoy, who was one of the bravest of the brave, was captured at the gun, after he had fired his last cartridge.

The Rev. Sam Chapman had passed through so many fights unscathed that the men had a superstition that he was as invulnerable as the son of Thetis. His hour had come at last, and a bullet pierced the celestial armor of the soldier-priest; but he fought with the rammer of his gun as he fell. He lived to pay the debt he contracted that day. "For time, at last, sets all things even." The victors now held the howitzer, and barred the only way for my escape; but I held in my hand a more potent talisman than Douglas threw into the Saracen ranks. My faith in the power of a six-shooter was as strong as the Crusader's was in the heart of the Bruce. I darted by the men who were now in possession of the gun, and received no hurt, except getting my face badly scratched by the limb of a tree as I passed. I had left Hoskins, Chapman, and Mountjoy in the hands of the enemy. Their shouts of triumph now rang through the woods; but no further pursuit was made. With a single companion, I stopped at a farmhouse, washed the blood from my face, and started back to get ready for another raid.

In a week I had rallied, and was down in Fairfax stirring up the outposts. Stuart sent me a message, that I might sell another gun for the same price. I had effected more than I had hoped.

When the news of my rout reached headquarters at Fairfax Court House, a flaming despatch (which is printed in Moore's "Rebellion Record") was sent North, announcing that "within two or three days Mosby had lost 150 men, and Gen. Stahel will not let him rest until his band is exterminated." As I had all the time acted on the offensive, it was easy enough for me to get rest by keeping quiet. As I had never had one-half that number of men, of course I could not have lost them. As long as I could keep a thousand men watching on the defensive for every one that I had with me, it was a small matter who got the best in a fight.

The Count of Paris, who was a staff officer in the Union army, in his history of the war, mentions the two affairs on the railroad, and says : "In Washington itself, Gen. Heintzelman was in command, who, beside the depots, the regiments under instruction, and the artillery in the forts, had under his control several thousand infantry ready to take the field, and Stahel's division of cavalry, numbering 6000 horses, whose only task was to pursue Mosby and the few hundred partisans led by this daring chief." If Pleasanton had had those 6000 sabres with him a few days after this, on June 9, 1863, in his great cavalry combat with Stuart at Brandy Station, the result might have been different. Hooker had asked for them, but had been refused, on the ground that they could not be spared from the defence of Washington.[1]

HEADQUARTERS, May 30, 1863.

STAHEL TO HEINTZELMAN : —

We had a hard fight with Mosby this morning, who had artillery, — the same which was used to destroy the train of cars. We whipped him like the devil, and took his artillery. My forces are still pursuing him. A more full report will follow, hoping the General will be satisfied with this result. JUL. STAHEL, *Major-General.*

Major-General Stahel reports of the above affair, that " The train for Bealeton had just passed up, and believing it to have been attacked, he [Col. Mann] immediately went with a detachment of the 5th N.Y. Cavalry, under command of Capt. A. H. Hasbrouck, a detachment of the 1st Vermont, under command of Lieut.-Col. Preston, and a small detachment of the 7th Michigan. The detachment of the 5th New York was sent directly across the country, in order to intercept the Rebels, while the balance of the command went directly to the scene of action. The advance of the 5th New York, led by Lieut. Elmer Barker, came up with the enemy first, and found them with the howitzer posted on a hill, with the cavalry drawn up in line in the rear to support it. Lieut. Barker, with his small detachment of about 25 men, dashed up the hill, and when within about 50 yards of the gun, received a charge of grape and canister, which killed three (3) and wounded seven (7) of our men, and several horses. The enemy then charged upon us, but were met with a stubborn resistance by the Lieutenant and his men, although the Lieutenant had received two grape-shots in his thigh. We were, however, overpowered and driven back a short distance. Just then Col. Preston of the 1st Vermont (Lieut. Hazleton, with companies H and C, being in advance) came up at a full charge upon their flank, and were received with a discharge from the howitzer of grape and canister. Our men pressed on, however, until they came to a hand-to-hand conflict, when the enemy gradually fell back. We took their howitzer, and they fled in every direction. . . . Our loss was four (4) killed, fifteen (15) wounded, the names of which please find enclosed. We also lost eleven (11) horses killed and several wounded."

CHAPTER XII.

" Fight as thy fathers fought,
     Fall as thy fathers fell!
Thy task is taught, thy shroud is wrought;
     So — forward — and farewell ! " — *Praed.*

I NOW turned my attention once more to the troops guarding the line of the Potomac and the defences of Washington.   I was afraid that if I continued my attacks on the railroad and in the vicinity of Hooker's camps, the cavalry division of Stahel would be released from doing guard duty, and sent to the front on the Rappahannock.[1]   So on June 3,

---

[1] In his testimony before the committee on the conduct of the war, Gen. Hooker says, vol. I, page 162:

" I may here state that while at Fairfax Court House my cavalry was reinforced by that of Maj.-Gen. Stahel.   The latter numbered 6100 sabres, and had been engaged in picketing a line from Occoquan River to Goose Creek.   This line was concentric to, and a portion of it within, the line held by my army.   The force opposed to them was Mosby's guerillas, numbering about 200 [not over thirty men]; and, if the reports of the newspapers were to be believed, this whole party was killed two or three times during the winter.   From the time I took command of the army of the Potomac there was no evidence that any force of the enemy, other than that above named, was within 100 miles of Washington City; and yet, the planks on the chain bridge were taken up at night during the greater part of the winter and spring. It was this cavalry force, it will be remembered, I had occasion to ask for, that my cavalry might be strengthened when it was numerically too weak to cope with the superior numbers of the enemy."

only three days after I had been routed and my howitzer captured near Greenwich, I collected thirty or
forty men and started once more for Fairfax. The
cavalry down there had enjoyed a season of rest for
several weeks. We passed by Fryingpan at night, and
slept in a thicket of pines on the Ox road. John Underwood was sent forward with a squad of men to fire
on the pickets or patrols. I knew that this would
draw out a force in search of us the next morning.
Just as I had got in a doze I heard several shots.
The men burst out laughing, and said, "That's John
Underwood." I had directed him to remain concealed by the roadside to watch for any scouting
party of the enemy that might come out in the
morning. About sunrise I received a message from
him that a body of about fifty cavalry had gone up
the road. In an instant we were all in our saddles;
but just then Underwood galloped up and informed
me that another body had passed on.

"How many do you think there are?"

"About 100," was his answer.

"All the better," I said; "we are in their rear. It
is just as easy to whip 100 as 50. Forward, trot!"

The party of the first part got to Fryingpan and
halted; we overtook the second party just as we got
in sight of the first. They were utterly confounded
at seeing a lot of men coming up on their rear, shoot·

ing and shouting.   They hadn't time to wheel around to meet an attack from behind, but broke and ran away.   They were driven pell-mell in a cloud of dust upon the body of cavalry that had halted at Frying-pan, and in turn they communicated the panic to their friends.   I came very near being caught here in the same trap that I got in at Warrenton Junction, but managed to get out without loss, beside carrying off a number of prisoners and horses.   Some of my men had chased the fugitives a few hundred yards when they unexpectedly came on a regiment of Federal cavalry drawn up in line just over a hill.   I have since ascertained that it was Col. Gray of the 6th Michigan cavalry.   He had come out on another road, and hearing the firing at Fryingpan, had formed to receive an attack.   If he had followed the example of Major Hammond with the 5th New York, at Warrenton Junction, and charged us when we were in disorder and scattered over the field, that would in all probability have been my last day as a partisan commander.   As soon as I heard of this third body of cavalry, which I had not seen, I drew off my men as rapidly as possible, while Col. Gray was waiting to receive us.   He managed to catch Dr. Alexander, who was with me.   I went off home with my spoil, and it was announced in Washington that I had once more been routed and driven away.   A few days after thæt I caught a Federal surgeon, and set him free on the condition that he would try to secure the release of Alexander. He kept his pledge.

As I have before stated, I had two months before this time received authority from the war department, through Gen. Lee, to raise a command. A good many men had joined me, but a considerable number of them had been captured at different times by raiding parties of the enemy. As it was the third year of the war the soldier element in the country had been pretty well exhausted by conscription, and I was forbidden to receive recruits from this class subject to conscript duty. It was, therefore, very difficult for me to get 60 eligible men, which was the legal standard for organizing a company. By this time I had about that number on my muster roll; but at least a third of them were in prison, having been captured at various times by raiding parties of the enemy. On June 10, 1863, my first company was organized at Rector Crossroads, with James W. Foster as captain, Thomas Turner of Maryland as 1st, William L. Hunter (now of California) as 2d, and George Whitescomer as 3d lieutenant. In compliance with law, I had to go through the form of an election. But I really appointed the officers, and told the men to vote for them. This was my rule as long as I had a command, and with two or three exceptions their conduct vindicated my judgment.   On the same day that the company was organized I started for the Potomac, as it was my policy to keep up a state of alarm about the capital.   I had long meditated crossing the river, but it was not fordable during the spring and winter season.   This was but a few weeks after the battle of Chancellorsville, and there was great fear at the North of a Confederate invasion.

Gen. Lee[1] was then moving up the Rappahannock

---

[1] The following correspondence between Gen. Pleasanton, chief of cavalry, and Gen. Ingalls, chief quartermaster of the army of the Potomac, which I recently found in the archives of the war department, shows the anxiety at that time to suppress my command. I had never heard of it before I saw it there.   It is evident that somebody had hoaxed Gen. Pleasanton, as the whole negotiation was confined to himself and Gen. Ingalls.   The fact that he had an unlimited amount of money placed at his disposal for buying me, and did not do it, is conclusive proof that there never had been a chance for it : —

HEADQUARTERS CAVALRY CORPS, June 12, 1863.

GEN. R. INGALLS, *Chief Quartermaster :* — Your despatch received. Ask the general how much of a bribe he can stand to get Mosby's services.   There is a chance for him; and just now he could do valuable service in the way of information, as well as humbugging the enemy. There's no news.   The rebels are like the boy the President tells about who stumped his toe and was too big to cry.   Birney is up.

A. PLEASANTON, *Brigadier-General.*

HEADQUARTERS ARMY OF THE POTOMAC,
June 12, 1863.

GEN. PLEASANTON : — If you think your scheme can succeed in regard to Mosby, do not hesitate as to the matter of money.   Use your own judgment, and do precisely what you think best for the public interest.   ROBERT INGALLS,
Brigadier-General.

on his way to Pennsylvania. I knew that if I only crossed over once, a small army would be detached to protect the border. Information had reached me that a squadron of Michigan cavalry was at Seneca; and I resolved to attack it. My plan was to cross the river at night, capture the patrols, and surprise the camp about daybreak.[1] Unfortunately, the night was very dark; my guide missed the way, and we did not get over the river until daybreak. I sent

---

[1] MIDDLEBURG, VA., June 10, 1863.

GENERAL: — I left our point of rendezvous yesterday for the purpose of making a night attack on two cavalry companies of the enemy on the Maryland shore. Had I succeeded in crossing the river at night, as I expected, I would have had no difficulty in capturing them; but, unfortunately, my guide mistook the road, and, instead of crossing by 11 o'clock at night, I did not get over until after daylight. The enemy (between 80 and 100 strong), being apprised of my movement, were formed to receive me. A charge was ordered, the shock of which the enemy could not resist; and they were driven several miles in confusion, with the loss of seven killed, a considerable number wounded, and 17 prisoners; also 20 odd horses or more. We burned their tents, stores, camp equipage, etc. I regret the loss of two brave officers killed — Capt. Brawner and Lieut. (George H.) Whitescarver. I also had one man wounded.

Respectfully your obedient servant,

JOHN S. MOSBY,
Major of Partisan Rangers.

MAJ.-GEN. J. E. B. STUART.

[*Indorsement.*]

HEADQUARTERS CAVALRY DIVISION, June 16, 1863.

Respectfully forwarded. In consideration of his brilliant services, I hope the President will promote Maj. Mosby.

J. E. B. STUART,
Major-General.

Alfred Glasscock, Joe Nelson, and Trunnell ahead, who concealed themselves in the bushes on the canal bank, and seized the patrol as it came along without giving any alarm. When I reached the northern bank they were waiting for me. The same party then went on up the towpath and captured a canal boat and some mules; while I halted a short time to close up the command. When we got near the bridge over the canal, we met another patrol, that fired and fled. They pulled up the drawbridge behind them; and it took us some minutes to replace it. This delay gave time to the cavalry in camp to saddle up. Before we got in 200 yards of them they retreated rapidly. After crossing a narrow bridge over Seneca Creek, they halted, and held it against a few of my men, who had pursued them. They were armed with carbines, and poured such a hot fire into the men that they started to fall back. Just then I rode up. Some of them were carrying Glasscock away, as he had been severely wounded.

After waiting a minute or two for my command to close up, we dashed across the bridge and completely routed the cavalry on the other bank. Frank String-fellow rode by my side as I led the charge, but we had hardly got over before George Whitescarver was ahead of us. The Michigan men broke and fled, leaving behind 17 prisoners, 30 horses, their colors, four dead and one wounded, beside all their camp equipage and stores. They had formed a line of a crescent shape not more than 50 yards from the bridge, on which they poured a converging fire, but not one of us was touched in going over. I had not gone a hundred yards in pursuit when Foster, who was riding by me, said, as we passed a dead man in the road: "There is one of our boys." He was so begrimed with dust that I did not recognize him. It was Whitescarver. The men were soon recalled. I was apprehensive that the enemy's cavalry on the river above might come down the towpath and intercept us. Then there was the danger, if I tarried too long in Maryland, that Maj.-Gen. Stahel would be ready to catch me on the Virginia shore, for his camps were only a few miles below. I was accompanied that day by Capt. Brawner, who commanded an independent company, and had come over to Fauquier a few days before. With two or three men he had kept on after I had abandoned the pursuit, and was killed.[1] I returned to Middleburg unmolested, wrote a despatch to Stuart, and forwarded my

---

[1] One who was in command at Poolesville, Md., a few miles from Seneca, reports: "About 250 of the enemy's cavalry crossed the Potomac near Muddy Branch at daybreak. The enemy dashed rapidly up the canal, driving in the patrols, and attacked Capt. Deane's company (I) 6th Michigan cavalry, on duty at Seneca locks. Capt. Deane fell back toward Poolesville, forming line three times, and only re-

prisoners. The next day I sent him the captured guidon, by Maj. White of his staff. The raid had all the effect I desired in arousing the fears of the enemy for the safety of the North.

Col. Thompson of the California cavalry battalion, who accompanied Col. Lowell in pursuit of me through Leesburg, recently informed me that when they got to Fairfax on their return they found Gen. Stahel's division prepared for battle. Stahel had sent out scouting parties over the country. I had no positive knowledge of the intention of Gen. Lee to invade the North, but all signs pointed that way. First came the news of Milroy's rout by Ewell at Winchester. As I was looking for Stuart every day, I made no more raids that week, but held my men ready to do any work that he wanted. On June 16 Stuart crossed the Rappahannock, and bivouacked near Piedmont station in Fauquier that night. On the same day I went with a few men on a scout in the neighborhood of Thoroughfare, to find out which way Hooker was moving. I saw from the smoke of his camp fires that he was retiring on Washington as Lee advanced toward the Potomac.

---

treating when nearly surrounded. The enemy followed to within three miles of Poolesville, when he rapidly retired, destroying the camp of Capt. Deane, and recrossing the river at the point where he had crossed. Our loss is four men killed, 16 men missing, one man wounded."

Early on the morning of the 17th I visited Stuart's headquarters at Miss Kitty Shacklett's house. As he was mounted on a very indifferent horse, I gave him a fine sorrel that one of my men had recently captured from a Michigan lieutenant. I told him what I knew about the position of the enemy, and that I was ready to perform any service he wanted. The cavalry moved on to Middleburg, and I met him there again in the afternoon. There were 30 or 40 of my men with me. He had never seen them before, and made some jocular remarks about them as they passed. We had a short conference, and he approved of the expedition on which I was going across the Potomac. There had been so many alarms along the enemy's lines that it was difficult for them to reinforce any one point more strongly than it had been; and I knew that they would now rely on the presence of Hooker's troops for the protection of Maryland. I did not think they were expecting me to come back to Seneca. My idea was to create a diversion in favor of Gen. Lee, who was marching into the Shenandoah valley, and also to keep him informed of the movement of the enemy. I bade Stuart "good by," and told him that he would soon hear from me. He had sent Wickham's brigade down to picket the gap in the Bull Run mountain at Aldie. His duty was to observe the enemy, and mask the movements of the Confederate army. My command turned off three miles above there, and moved again toward Seneca. It was a very hot day, and we had stopped a while to rest under the shade of some trees, and refresh ourselves with buttermilk at the house of a farmer named Gulick. Presently we heard artillery firing over toward Aldie, which indicated a collision of the enemy's cavalry with ours. In an instant every man was mounted. From a commanding position on the mountain, which we reached in a few minutes, I could see clouds of dust rising on every road, which showed that Hooker was marching for the Potomac. After going a little farther, we captured a number of prisoners, and I immediately sent a despatch to Stuart, with the information I got from them. I could not now get to Seneca without passing through Hooker's infantry, so I concluded to go down on the Little River turnpike, and operate on the line of communication between Pleasanton's cavalry and the general headquarters. I knew I could gather some prizes there, and probably keep Stahel's cavalry from coming to the front, by giving them plenty to do in their rear. So we kept ourselves concealed, like Robin Hood and his merry men, in the green wood until night, and then sallied out in quest of **game.** After it was dark, we moved to a point about four miles below Aldie, where Pleasanton and Rosser had been fighting, and on the pike leading to Fairfax Court House, near which Hooker's headquarters were established that evening. My command was now inside of Hooker's lines, and environed on all sides by the camps of his different corps. Along the pike a continuous stream of troops, with all the impedimenta of war, poured along. Taking three men with me — Joe Nelson, Charlie Hall, and Norman Smith — I rode out into the column of Union troops as they passed along. As it was dark, they had no suspicion who we were, although we were all dressed in full Confederate uniform. A man by the name of Birch lived in a house near the roadside, and I discovered three horses standing at his front gate, with a man holding them by their bridles. I was sure that he was an orderly, and that they were officers' horses. We rode up, and asked him to whom they belonged. He replied that they were Maj. Stirling's and Capt. Fisher's, and that they were just from Gen. Hooker's headquarters. I then called him up to me and took him by the collar, and leaning down, whispered in his ear: "You are my prisoner. My name is Mosby." The man, who was an Irishman, understood me to say that he was "Mosby," and indignantly replied, "You are a d—d liar. I am as good a Union man as you are." Just then in the starlight he saw the gleam of a pistol, and had nothing further to say.

In a few minutes the officers came out of the house. I saluted them, and asked which way they were going and where they were from. As we seemed to be in such friendly relations with their orderly, they never suspected our hostile character, and promptly answered that they were from Gen. Hooker's headquarters, and were carrying despatches to Pleasanton. Capt. Fisher was his chief signal officer, going up to establish a signal station at Snicker's gap — if he could get there. By this time my men had dismounted, and as I was talking to Maj. Stirling, Joe Nelson walked up, and, politely extending his hand, asked for his pistol. Charlie Hall, not to be outdone in courtesy by Joe, proposed to relieve Capt. Fisher of his. They both misunderstood what Hall and Nelson meant, and offered to shake hands with them. In an instant the barrels of four glittering revolvers informed them that death was their doom if they refused to be prisoners. Resistance was useless and they surrendered. All now mounted quickly and we left the pike. As we started, both officers burst out laughing. I asked them what they were laughing at. They said they had laughed so much about their people being gobbled up by me that they were now enjoying the joke being turned on themselves. They were then informed that I knew that they had despatches for Pleasanton, and that they could relieve me of performing a disagreeable duty by handing them over. Maj. Stirling promptly complied. I then went to a farmer's house near by, got a light, and read them.[1] They contained just such information as Gen. Lee wanted, and were the " open sesame " to Hooker's army. I wrote a note to Stuart to go with the despatches, which were sent with the prisoners under charge of Norman Smith. He got to Stuart's headquarters about daybreak. The skies were red that night in every direction with the light of the fires of the Union army. We slept soundly

---

[1] Stuart's report of the Gettysburg campaign says: " Maj. Mosby, with his usual daring, penetrated the enemy's lines and caught a staff officer of Gen. Hooker — bearer of despatches to Gen. Pleasanton, commanding United States cavalry near Aldie. These despatches disclosed the fact that Hooker was looking to Aldie with solicitude, and that Pleasanton, with infantry and cavalry, occupied the place; and that a reconnoissance in force of cavalry was meditated toward Warrenton and Culpepper. I immediately despatched to Gen. Hampton, who was coming by way of Warrenton from the direction of Beverly ford, this intelligence, and directed him to meet this advance at Warrenton. The captured despatches also gave the entire number of divisions, from which we could estimate the approximate strength of the enemy's army. I therefore concluded in no event to attack with cavalry alone the enemy at Aldie. . . . Hampton met the enemy's advance toward Culpepper and Warrenton, and drove him back without difficulty — a heavy storm and night intervening to aid the enemy's retreat."

within a mile of Birney's corps at Gum Spring, and in the morning began operations on the pike. We soon got as many fish in our nets as we could haul out, and then returned into the Confederate lines. Stuart was delighted to see me; he had also learned from the captured despatches that a cavalry reconnoissance would be sent to Warrenton the next day. Notice of it was sent to Gen. Hampton, who met and repulsed it.

After a series of indecisive engagements, extending through several days, Pleasanton, finally, on the 21st of June, supported by a force of infantry, drove Stuart back to Ashby's Gap in the Blue Ridge. Having effected the object of his reconnoissance, which was to ascertain the position of the Confederate army that was then moving down the Shennandoah Valley, Pleasanton retired on the same night to Aldie, where the 5th Corps was posted, and did not again assume the offensive as long as Hooker remained in Virginia. He stood on the defensive and simply watched and waited. On the next day, Stuart re-established his lines about Middleburg, with his headquarters at Rector's Crossroads, where he kept up communication with Gen. Lee, who was at Berryville. Hill and Longstreet were near there, and Ewell had gone into Maryland. On the afternoon when Pleasanton followed the Con-

federate cavalry through Upperville to the mountain,
I was with my command on Dulony's farm, about
a mile from the pike, as he passed. I determined
again to strike at his rear. As we were passing
Bull Run mountain by a narrow path that night,
one of my men, about the middle of the column,
dropped his hat, and stopped to pick it up. It was
pitch dark; and, as those in front of him knew nothing about it, they kept on. The men behind him
halted. This cut my column in two; and half of
it wandered all night in the woods, but never found
me. We slept in a drenching rain on the top of the
mountain, and started early in the morning. As we
were going through Dr. Ewell's farm, I stopped to
talk with him; but the men went on. Presently, I
saw them halt near a church in the woods; and one
of them beckoned to me. I galloped up, and saw a
body of about thirty cavalry drawn up not a hundred
yards in front of us. I instantly ordered a charge;
and, just as we got upon them, they ran away, while
a heavy fire was poured into us by a company of
infantry concealed in the church. A negro had carried the news of our being on the mountain to Gen.
Meade, who had prepared this ambuscade for me.
Three of my men — Charlie Hall, Mountjoy, and
Ballard — were wounded; the latter losing a leg.
The lieutenant commanding the Federal cavalry

was killed. I was not ten steps from the infantry when they fired the volley. We fell back to the mountain ; and, no doubt, Gen. Meade thought that I was done for — at least for that day. After taking care of my wounded, I started again for the Little River Pike, which we reached by flanking Gen. Meade. Pretty soon we caught a train of twenty wagons, and proceeded to unhitch the mules. I did not have more than one man to a wagon. The guard to the train rallied, and recaptured some of the animals, and two of my men ; but we got away with most of them. That night they were delivered to Stuart's quartermaster. This raid is a fine illustration of the great results that may be achieved by a partisan force co-operating with the movements of an army. My principal aim in these operations was to get information for Stuart, and, by harassing the communications of the Federal army, to neutralize with my small command Stahel's three brigades of cavalry in Fairfax.[1]

---

[1] Gen. Stahel, in a report to the secretary of war, says that on June 21 he received an order from Hooker's headquarters to make a reconnoissance in force to Warrenton and the upper Rappahannock. " In compliance with this order," he says, " I started with my command for Warrenton and the upper Rappahannock. Just as I was about crossing the Rappahannock with two brigades, — one of my brigades being already across, — for the purpose of executing the above orders, and to break up Gen. Lee's communication with Richmond, and which could have been easily effected, as there were but very few troops,

It happened that on June 22 — the very day we captured the wagon train — Gen. Stahel, in obedience to Hooker's orders, had gone from Fairfax with three cavalry brigades and a battery of artillery, on a reconnoissance to the Rappahannock. On June 23, just as one of his brigades had crossed over the river, and the other two were in the act of crossing, he received an order from Gen. Hooker to return immediately, and to dispose his force so as to catch the party inside his lines that had captured his wagon train. We had got to Stuart's headquarters with Hooker's mules before Stahel got the

---

and Gen. Lee's rear consisting of their cavalry, with which Gen. Pleasanton was engaged in the upper part of the valley, received the following order from Hooker:

"'JUNE 23.

"'MAJ.-GEN. HANCOCK: — Direct Gen. Stahel to return without delay; to dispose his forces so as to catch the party inside our lines, if possible.'

"Another despatch stated that the force was about 100; that they attacked one of our trains on the Aldie road.

"It was with feelings of bitter regret and disappointment that I received this order, inasmuch as I was just crossing the Rappahannock with three brigades of cavalry and a battery of horse artillery, who were just fresh from camp, etc. . . . All of Lee's supplies had to pass up between the Rappahannock and Blue Ridge mountains or cross to the Shenandoah valley; and my force was sufficient to have destroyed his entire trains and to cut off Gen. Lee completely from his supplies. . . . I was compelled by this order to abandon my movement, and restrained from dealing so fatal a blow to the enemy, and return with my whole division to disperse about 100 guerillas who had escaped back out of our lines before I ever received the order to return."

order. He did not come there to search for them. If he had not been recalled, he might have done much damage on Gen. Lee's line of communication, as it was entirely uncovered. In fact, there was no Confederate force between him and Richmond. When afterward, Gen. Hooker, before the committee on the conduct of the war, criticised the authorities at Washington so severely for keeping this large force to watch my small one, he had forgotten that he had done the same thing himself.[1] In a letter to Stuart, dated June 23, 1863, 5 P.M., Gen. Lee refers with some uneasiness to this expedition of Stahel. He did not know at the time that Stahel had gone back. In an interview I had with Stuart on my return, we discussed the best route for him to go into Maryland. As I knew all the roads, as well as the location of each corps of the enemy, that were all wide apart, I thought he ought to go through an unguarded gap of the Bull Run mountain, and, cutting his way right through the middle

---

[1] [*Telegram.*]

GAINSVILLE, 11 A.M., June 23, 1863.

STAHEL to BUTTERFIELD, *Chief of Staff to Hooker :* Your order to return without delay received through Maj.-Gen. Hancock, after midnight; made arrangements at once, and my advance arrived here from Warrenton this morning at 8 o'clock. . . . In accordance with your order, I shall scout the whole country, from Bull Run mountain toward Fairfax Court House, and have ordered the rest of my command and my train to Fairfax, where I shall report personally to you.

of the Union army, cross the Potomac at Seneca.[1] It was the shortest route he could go into Maryland, and there was a splendid opportunity to destroy Hooker's transportation as he went along, and to cut off communication between Washington and the North. The plan was at that time perfectly practicable. Hooker was in a defensive attitude, waiting the development of Lee's plans, and only a small portion of the cavalry was necessary to be held in our front to observe the enemy and report their movements to the commanding general. The plan was to leave two brigades of cavalry about Middleburg to do this work, while Stuart, with three brigades, should pass through Hooker's army into Maryland. The brigades selected to be left behind were those of Jones and Beverly H. Robertson, under command of the latter, who happened to be the ranking officer. They numbered over 3000 men, and exceeded in strength the three that Stuart took with him.

As Hancock's corps was holding Hopewell and Thoroughfare gaps, the road that Stuart determined to go was through Glasscock's gap (a few miles south of Thoroughfare) via Haymarket, through Loudoun

---

[1] It now appears from their correspondence that Stuart, Longstreet, and Gen. Lee had already been discussing the feasibility of his going this route.

to Seneca ford on the Potomac. The part assigned to me was to cross the Bull Run at night by the bridle path I had so frequently travelled, and, uniting with Stuart near Gum Spring in Loudoun, take command of his advance guard. Hooker's headquarters were still at Fairfax station, with his army spread out like a fan over Loudoun, Prince William and Fairfax counties, his left being at Thoroughfare, his right at Leesburg, with his centre at Aldie, and Pleasanton's cavalry in front of it. Stuart's plan, of course, contemplated his crossing of the river in advance of Hooker or Lee, and opening communication with Ewell as soon as he was over. During our interview Gen. Hampton and Fitz Lee came into the room, and soon afterward Stuart started a courier off to Gen. Lee. I have been informed by one of his staff that he rode over to Berryville that day to have a personal interview with the commanding general. Before we parted, he told me that Gen. Lee was very apprehensive that Hooker would steal a march and get into Maryland ahead of him, and asked me to go and find out if any portion of his army was crossing the river. Although I had been almost continuously in the saddle for three days and nights, I agreed to return inside of Hooker's lines. With only two men I crossed the Bull Run again that night, and early the next morning was riding in full Confederate uniform through the Union army.

I soon sent Stuart a despatch that I was certain Hooker's army was not in motion. Proceeding some distance down the pike with my single companion, we had stopped to talk with a citizen, when four lieutenants belonging to the 3d corps, that was camped near by, walked up to us. There was a drizzling rain, and we had waterproofs thrown over our shoulders. As they were in full view of their camps, they had no suspicion of danger and were without arms. After talking with them for some minutes, they were stunned by a demand for their surrender. I sent them back under guard of one man, with another despatch to Stuart. I then rode on alone down into Fairfax, where I met some of my old acquaintances, who thought when they first saw me that it was my ghost.

Having learned all about the situation of Hooker's army, I started back. I stopped at the house of John I. Coleman to inquire the shortest way to the pike. It was the first time he ever saw me, and, although I showed him my gray uniform and star, he thought I was trying to play a Yankee trick on him, and refused to tell me anything. While we were talking, I heard a noise behind me. Turning around, I saw two mounted men approaching us.

When within about fifty yards, they stopped, and be· gan picking cherries from a tree. I drew my pistol, but kept it under my gum cloth, and rode up to them. They never suspected that I was an enemy. I asked them where they were from; they answered that they were on duty with Reynolds' corps that was camped near by at Guilford. They had no arms; so, of course, had to surrender. When Coleman saw this affair, he was more convinced than ever that I was a Yankee dressed up in gray. I had to get to the pike the best way I could. So I tied the heads of my prisoners' horses together with their halters, to keep them from running away, and went on.

It was near sunset when I came in sight of the pike, about four miles below Aldie. There was a wagon train a mile or so in length passing on the road, with a strong cavalry guard, that was carrying supplies to the troops above. I was anxious to get to Stuart that night, and knew that if I waited for the train to pass, it would be dark, and I could not find the mountain path. So I drew my pistol, held it under cover, and told my prisoners that if they spoke a word they would be dead men. I then rode, with them by my side, through a gap in the fence into the pike, right among the Union cavalry. We could not cross over at that point, as the fence on the other side of the road was too high for our horses to leap. We went along for 200 yards, with my prisoners, through the wagon train and cavalry escort, until we got to a road leading away from the pike. Here we turned off. The gum cloth I had over my shoulders to protect me from the rain, as it did not cover one-third of my body, did not conceal the uniform I wore. I had ridden through the ranks of a column of Union cavalry in broad daylight, with two prisoners, and my elbow had actually struck against one as I passed. In doing so I had acted on the maxim of Danton *de l'Audace, toujours audace.* Finding that I could not reach the mountain before night, and fearing to go to sleep in the woods alone with my prisoners, I took their paroles and sent them back to their friends. Of course, I kept their horses. Early the next morning I was again at Stuart's headquarters.[1]

---

[1] Stuart's report says: " . . . I resumed my own position now, at Rector's cross roads, and being in constant communication with the commanding general, had scouts busily employed watching and reporting the enemy's movements, and reporting the same to the commanding general. In this difficult search the fearless and indefatigable Maj. Mosby was particularly active and efficient. His information was always accurate and reliable."

CHAPTER XIII.

STUART had now received his final instructions
from General Lee, authorizing him to move into
Maryland, around the rear of the enemy and between
him and Washington.   He was likewise instructed
to do them all the damage he could on his way.
With his transportation destroyed and communications broken, Hooker would be seriously embarrassed
in pursuing General Lee, or probably forced to fall
back for supplies, or to defend the capital against
this demonstration.   In the meantime, while Hooker
was thus delayed, the Confederates would have been
levying contributions on the farmers in Pennsylvania.   His original plan, which was bold in conception and perfectly practicable in execution, was
thwarted by an event which he could not control.
It was obvious now that Hooker would not *initiate*
any movement, but would confine himself to covering
the capital and observing his adversary.   It was
equally plain that when the Confederate army made
a move west of the Blue Ridge, Hooker would make
a corresponding one on the east.   It was, therefore,
all important for the success of Stuart's movement
that the *status quo* of the two armies should be pre-

served until he could get through Hooker's army to
the river, when it would be too late for Hooker to
take any step to defeat it.   The distance was not
more than twenty miles to the Potomac from the point
where he would enter Hooker's lines ; and this could
be got over between sunrise and sundown, as he intended to march in three parallel columns.   He knew
the country well, and the position of each corps ; and
it would have been easy enough for him to flank them.
Before Pleasanton could have got ready to follow the
blazing meteor, it would have been out of sight.
The three brigades that were to accompany Stuart
were quietly withdrawn from Pleasanton's front on
the evening of June 24, and marched in a southerly
direction to their rendezvous at Salem.   Those of
Jones and Robertson were put in the position they
had held about Middleburg, and, of course, were
charged with the ordinary duty of cavalry on a post
of observation.   As Gen. Stuart says in his report, "*Robertson's and Jones's brigades, under command of the former, were left in observation of the
enemy, on the usual front (about Middleburg), with
full instructions as to following of the enemy, in case
of withdrawal, and joining our main army.*"   An
order to a cavalry officer to *observe* an enemy, of
course implies that he is to report what he sees ;
otherwise, there is no use in his observing.   Stuart
left behind a force of over 3000 cavalry, which

was amply sufficient for every purpose. By day-break, on the morning of the 25th, his column debouched through Glassock's Gap, in the Bull Run, and proceeded towards Haymarket. At the same time I started across by the route I had been travelling for a week, to connect with him at the appointed place. We had stopped at a spring on the mountain side to make our breakfast on some sutlers' stores that had been saved from our cap-tives. Two men had been sent forward on a picket; but they had scarcely got a hundred yards before a volley was fired; and the bullets whistled all around us. We sprang upon our horses; but, as the men did not return, we knew that they must have been killed or captured. General Meade, whose camps were near by, had prepared an am-buscade a second time for me, but I had escaped. (I wonder if he would have called this *bushwhack-ing.*) We made a *detour* around them, and hurried on to join Stuart; as we could hear his cannon about Haymarket. It seems that when Stuart got there, he found the roads on which he intended to march that day occupied by Hancock's corps, that had broken up camp that morning, and was moving towards the Potomac. When I got to the Little River Pike, about eight miles below Aldie, which was to be our point of junction, instead of meeting him we struck the head of Hancock's column. His

divisions were marching on every road. I spent the
day and night riding about among them, and with
great difficulty extricated myself from the dilemma
in which I was placed. I could not find out where
Stuart was, nor he where I was ; for Hancock was
between us. So I retraced my steps and went on
to Pennsylvania through the Shenandoah Valley,
passing General Robertson's command, that was
quietly resting in Ashby's and Snicker's Gaps, in
the Blue Ridge, after the enemy retired on the
26th. Pleasanton that day had moved by his flank,
across General Robertson's front, to Leesburg, to
cover the crossing of Hooker's army. Why he
should have halted and remained idle three days
in the gaps of the Blue Ridge in Virginia after
both armies had marched into Pennsylvania is a
mystery that has never been satisfactorily explained.
If there were any sound military reasons for his
staying there *three* days, there were equally as sound
ones for his not leaving at all. His proper position
was on General Lee's flank, next to the enemy, in
order to protect his rear and to keep him informed of
their movement.

If General Robertson had then in obedience to
General Lee's and Stuart's instructions, promptly
followed the enemy along the base of South Mountain through Boonsboro, the Confederate cavalry
might easily have reached Gettysburg in advance of

the Federal troops. In this event, there would **not** have been the accidental collision of armies. General Lee would have fought a defensive battle, and Gettysburg might have been to Southern hearts something more than "a glorious field of grief." Even as it was, Stuart's movement around his rear had so confused General Meade, that his army was more scattered than ours, and two of his corps in the first day's fight, were caught *in delicto* and crushed. He was looking for Lee on the Susquehanna, when in fact he was concentrating on Gettysburg.

On account of Hancock's unexpected movement, Stuart had been compelled to make a wider circuit than he had intended, and did not cross the Potomac until the night of the twenty-seventh, the day after Hooker got over. He thence moved northerly towards the Susquehanna, to put himself on Ewell's flank in accordance with the instructions of General Lee. But owing to the derangement of his plans by the advance of the Union army, without General Robertson having given him notice of it, Ewell had been recalled, and Stuart did not join the army until July the second, at Gettysburg, when the battle was raging. But Robertson's command had not even then come up. This movement of Stuart's around the rear of Hooker's army has been condemned by General Long, the military secretary and biographer of General Lee, as having been undertaken either "from misapprehension of his instructions, or love of the éclat of a bold raid" (which, of course, implies disobedience of orders) ;[1] and General Long-street says that as he was leaving the Blue Ridge, he instructed Stuart to follow him down the Valley, and cross the Potomac at Shepherdstown, but that Stuart replied that he had discretionary powers from General Lee where to cross the Potomac.

When this charge was made against Stuart, both the critics were viewing his movement in the light of

---

[1] In the "Memoirs of General Lee," p. 271, General Long says: " Previous to the passage of the Potomac, General Stuart was instructed to make the movements of the cavalry correspond with those of the Federal army, so that he might be in position to observe and report all important information. In the performance of this duty Stuart had never failed, and probably his great confidence in him made Lee less specific in his instructions than he would otherwise have been. But on this occasion either from the misapprehension of instructions or the love of the éclat of a bold raid, Stuart, instead of maintaining his appropriate position between the armies, placed himself on the right flank of the enemy, where his communication with Lee was effectually severed. This greatly embarrassed the movements of General Lee, and eventually forced him to an engagement under disadvantageous circumstances."

In the Century Magazine, General Longstreet, in his article on Gettysburg, says: " When Hill with his troops and well-supplied trains had passed my rear, I was ordered to withdraw from the Blue Ridge, pass over to the west of the Shenandoah and to follow the movements of the other troops, only to cross the Potomac at Williamsport. I ordered Gen. Stuart, whom I considered under my command, to occupy the gaps with a part of his cavalry and to follow with his main force on my right, to cross the Potomac at Shepherdstown, and move on my right flank. Upon giving him this order, he informed me that he had authority from Gen. Lee to occupy the gaps with a part of his cavalry, and to follow the Federal army with the remainder. At the same time he expressed his purpose of crossing the river east of the Blue Ridge the disaster to our arms at Gettysburg, and it **was** more agreeable to put the blame of it on a dead **man** than a living one.   General Long, who had access to the Confederate archives, may plead the blindness with which he is afflicted as an excuse for his error, and I have no doubt that General Longstreet has forgotten that his own letter to Stuart contradicts his statement.

Gen. Lee made two reports of this campaign;

---

and trying to make way around the right of the Federal army; so I moved my troops independent of the cavalry, following my orders, crossed at Williamsport, come up with A. P. Hill in Maryland, and we moved on thence to Chambersburg." . . . "On the 30th of June we turned our faces toward our enemy and marched upon Gettysburg. The third corp, under Hill, moved out first, and my command followed. We then found ourselves in a very unusual condition: we were almost in the immediate presence of the enemy with our cavalry gone.   Stuart was undertaking another wild ride around the Federal army.   We knew nothing of Meade's movements further than the report my scout had made.   We did not know, except by surmises, when or where to expect to find Meade, nor whether he was lying in wait or advancing." Gen. Longstreet will find it difficult to reconcile what he now says were his orders to the cavalry with his letter to Stuart, or the following one to Gen. Lee:

HEADQUARTERS, June 22, 1863, 7.30 P.M.

GEN. R. E. LEE,
    Comdg., &c.

GENERAL : — Yours of 4 O'C. this afternoon is rec'd.   I have forwarded your letters to Gen. Stuart with the suggestion that he pass *by the enemy's rear,* if he thinks that he may get through.   We have nothing of the enemy to-day.   Most respectfully,

J. LONGSTREET,
Lt.-Genl., Comdg.

So it appears that it was Gen. Longstreet who suggested to Stuart the idea of " another wild ride around the Federal army," one written in July, 1863, a few weeks after the battle; and a more detailed one in January, 1864. There is a slight color of truth in the imputation cast upon Stuart that Gen. Lee intended to censure him in his report. But this is owing to a false interpretation given to it by persons who have construed a single sentence literally, and not in connection with others that qualify and explain it.[1] Gen. Lee does say:

---

[1] General Lee says: " In the meantime, the progress of Ewell, who was already in Maryland with Jenkin's cavalry, advanced into Pennsylvania as far as Chambersburg, rendered it necessary that the rest of the army should be within supporting distance, and Hill having reached the Valley, Longstreet was withdrawn to the west side of the Shenandoah, and the two corps encamped near Berryville.

" General Stuart was directed to hold the mountain-passes with part of his command *as long as the enemy remained south of the Potomac,* and with the *remainder* to cross into Maryland and place himself on the right of General Ewell. Upon the suggestion of the former officer, that he could damage the enemy and delay his passage of the river by getting in his rear, he was authorized to do so, and it was left to his discretion whether to enter Maryland east or west of the Blue Ridge; but he was instructed to lose no time in placing his command on the right of our column as soon as he perceived the enemy moving northward.

*　　*　　*　　*　　*　　*　　*　　*

" It was expected that as soon as the Federal army should cross the Potomac, General Stuart would give notice of its movements ; and, nothing having been heard from him since our entrance into Maryland, it was inferred that the enemy had not left Virginia. Orders were therefore issued to move on Harrisburg.

"The expedition of General Early to York was designed in part to prepare for this undertaking, by breaking the railroad between Baltimore and Harrisburg, and seizing the bridge over the Susquehanna at Wrightsville.

*　　*　　*　　*　　*　　*　　*　　*

"The advance against Harrisburg was arrested by intelligence received from a scout on the night of the 28th, to the effect that the

" It was expected that as soon as the Federal army
should cross the Potomac, *Gen. Stuart* would give
notice of its movements, and nothing having been
heard from him since our entrance into Maryland, it
was inferred that the enemy had not yet left Virginia.
Orders were therefore issued to move on Harrisburg."
Now if all that Gen. Lee says in his report about

---

army of General Hooker had crossed the Potomac and was approaching the mountains. In the absence of the cavalry it was impossible
to ascertain his intentions; but to deter him from advancing farther
west and intercepting our communications with Virginia, it was determined to concentrate the army east of the mountains.

*   *   *   *   *   *   *   *

" The movement of the army preceding the battle of Gettysburg had
been much embarrassed by the absence of the cavalry. As soon as
it was known that the enemy had crossed into Maryland, orders were
sent to the brigades of [B. H.] Robertson and [Wm. E.] Jones,
which had been left to guard the passes of the Blue Ridge, to rejoin
the army *without delay*, and it was expected that General Stuart, with
the *remainder* of his command, would soon arrive. In the exercise
of the discretion given him when Longstreet and Hill marched into
Maryland, General Stuart determined to pass around the rear of the
Federal army, with three brigades, and cross the Potomac between it
and Washington, believing that by that route he would be able to
place himself on our right flank in time to keep us properly advised
of the enemy's movements. He marched from Salem on the night
of June 24th, intending to pass west of Centreville, but found the
enemy's forces so distributed as to render that route impracticable.
Adhering to his original plan, he was forced to make a wide detour
through Buckland and Brentsville, and crossed the Occoquan at Wolf
Run Shoals on the morning of the 27th. Continuing his march
through Fairfax Court House and Drainesville, he arrived at the Potomac below the mouth of Seneca Creek in the evening. He found
the river much swollen by the recent rains, but after great exertion
gained the Maryland shore, before midnight, with his whole command.
He now ascertained that the whole Federal army, which he had discovered to be drawing towards the Potomac, had crossed the day be-

Stuart's cavalry is read, together *as a whole*, it is apparent that in the sentence above quoted, he uses *Stuart's* name not in a personal sense, but descriptive of his cavalry corps, for in another place he says that Stuart had been directed to divide his cavalry, leaving a portion to watch the enemy in front of the mountain passes in Virginia, and " with the *remainder* to cross into Maryland and place himself on the right of Gen. Ewell," who was marching on Harrisburg.[1]

Clearly Gen. Lee did not intend to involve himself in the contradiction of saying that he expected Stuart *personally* to perform at the same time the double duty of watching Hooker along the Potomac,

---

fore, and was moving towards Fredericktown, thus interposing itself between him and our forces.

* * * * * * * *

" Robertson's and Jones's brigades arrived on July 3d, and were stationed upon our right flank. The severe loss sustained by the army, and the reduction of its ammunition, rendered another attempt to dislodge the enemy inadvisable, and it was therefore determined upon to withdraw."

[1] Stuart has been criticised for carrying into our lines a train of one hundred and twenty-five wagons, which he captured in Maryland, with supplies for Hooker, on account of the delay it produced in joining Gen. Lee. But the expedition has been condemned, not as an independent raid, but because it is said that it deprived Gen. Lee of his cavalry, which ought to have given him notice of Hooker's advance into Pennsylvania. But as Gen. Lee actually received notice of it on the very night that Stuart crossed the Potomac, it is hard to see what harm was done by taking the wagons with him. And I have shown that Stuart left with Gen. Lee sufficient cavalry to do the work of guarding his flank and observing the enemy.

and guarding Ewell's flank on the Susquehanna.[1]
Gen. Lee in thus referring to Stuart was somewhat
careless and inaccurate in his language, as he was
when, in describing the battle of Gettysburg, he said
that Robertson's command *arrived* on July 3d,
when, in fact, it never got nearer than Cashtown,
some eight miles from the battle-field. But Gen.
Lee is explicit in saying, *in his report*, that he gave
Stuart full authority to make the movement around
the enemy's rear. Among the Confederate archives
in Washington, I have at last found in Gen. Lee's
confidential letter-book his final instructions to Stuart,
which have never been published, which must set
this controverted question at rest forever. At the
time when they were written, Gen. Lee's headquarters were at Berryville. They are dated June
23, 1863, 5 P.M.

In them Gen. Lee presents to Stuart the alternative of crossing the Potomac west of the Blue Ridge
at Shepherdstown and moving over to Frederick, Md.,
or, "*you will, however, be able to judge whether you
can pass around their army without hindrance, doing*

---

[1] So far as keeping Gen. Lee informed of Hooker's movements is
concerned, it was immaterial whether Stuart crossed east or west of
the Ridge. In either event he would have been separated from Gen.
Lee and unable to watch the line of the Potomac. Stuart was *ordered*
to take three brigades to the Susquehanna and to leave two behind
him to watch Hooker. He was simply given discretion as to the point
of crossing the Potomac. He is not responsible for the division of his
command.

*them all the damage you can, and cross the river east
of the mountains. In either case, after crossing the
river, you must move on and feel the right of Ewell's
troops, collecting information, provisions, etc."* In a
letter to Stuart dated June 22, he had said: *"If you
find that he is moving northward, and that two brigades can guard the Blue Ridge and take care of your
rear, you can move with the other three into Maryland
and take position on General Ewell's right, place yourself in communication with him, guard his flank and
keep him informed of the enemy's movements, and collect all the supplies you can for the use of the army.
One column of General Ewell's army will probably
move towards the Susquehanna by the Emmetsburg
route, another by Chambersburg."* The intention of
General Lee clearly was that Stuart with one portion
of the cavalry was to guard Ewell's flank and give
him information of the enemy. The other was to be
left[1] behind, as he says in his report, "to hold the

---

[1] On June 22, 1863, 3.30 P.M. Gen. Lee, writing from Berryville,
Va., to Ewell, who was then about Hagerstown, Md., says:

"My letter of to-day, authorizing you to move toward the Susquehanna, I hope has reached you ere this. I have also directed Gen.
Stuart, should the enemy have so far retired from his front as to permit of the departure of a portion of the cavalry, to march with three
brigades across the Potomac, and place himself on your right and in
communication with you, keep *you advised of the movements of the
enemy*, and assist in collecting supplies for the army. I have not
heard from him since." As Stuart was not ubiquitous, Gen. Lee must
have relied on the cavalry left behind to do for him what he intended
that Stuart should do for Ewell.

mountain passes *as long as the enemy remained south of the Potomac.*" To suppose that Gen. Lee intended them to remain there after the enemy had gone is to suppose that he was not only unfit to command an army, but even a corporal's guard. It is clear that he intended the two brigades under Robertson to perform the same service for the column of Longstreet and Hill (with whom he had his headquarters) as Stuart was to do for Ewell, who was separated from him. When these two corps crossed the Potomac on the 25th, *he knew* that Stuart had not crossed *west* of the Ridge in advance of them. He would not have committed the blunder of marching all his infantry into Pennsylvania knowing that all his cavalry was in Virginia. He must, therefore, have expected for Stuart to cross the Potomac on the same day to the *east* of the Ridge ; which he would have done but for Hancock's movement. Some have contended that his anxious inquiries for Stuart when he got to Chambersburg prove that he did not know which way he had gone. They only show that he did not know where Stuart was *at that time.* As Stuart had been directed to open communication, as soon as he got into Pennsylvania, with Ewell, and had not been able to do so on account of the Federal army getting between them, Gen. Lee, not having heard from him, very naturally felt a great deal of solicitude for his safety. If Gen. Lee had not thought that he would cross the Potomac somewhere on the same day that he did, he would have waited and sent for him. But again, Gen. Lee would not assume the responsibility of authorizing Stuart to go around Hooker's rear unless the movement had the approval of Gen. Longstreet, whose headquarters were at Millwood, not far from Berryville. Gen. Lee's instructions to Stuart were therefore sent through Longstreet. In a letter to Stuart, Longstreet not only approves of Stuart's going into Maryland around the rear of the enemy, but *opposes* his going the other route through the Shenandoah Valley, on the ground that it would disclose their plans to the enemy. In concluding his letter he says :

"*N.B. — I think that your passage of the Potomac by our rear at the present moment will in a measure disclose our plans. You had better not leave us, therefore, unless you can take the proposed route in rear of the enemy.*" By "*our rear*" Longstreet meant through the Shenandoah Valley. The reasons he gave Stuart were conclusive in favor of the course he took. It was Gen. Lee's policy to detain Hooker as long as possible in Virginia. But if Stuart passed to the west of the Ridge and crossed the Potomac at Shepherdstown, he would be discovered by the signal stations of the enemy on Maryland heights. This would indicate, of course, that the infantry was to follow him. On the contrary, Hooker would interpret a movement around his rear as nothing more than a cavalry *raid*, and it would be a mask to conceal Lee's designs. It was no fault of Stuart's that he was unable to execute his plan.

The Count of Paris says that it was impracticable from the first, and differed in its condition from his other operations of this kind, because they were undertaken while the armies were both stationary. Now, at the time when Stuart resolved on going into Maryland by this route, both armies were as stationary as when he rode around McClellan on the Chickahominy; and Hooker was waiting for the Confederates to move. But it could not be expected for Hooker to stand still while his adversary was in motion. Now it so happened that the corps of Longstreet and Hill moved from Berryville on June 24, towards the Potomac, which they crossed the next day, Hill at Shepherdstown, and Longstreet at Williamsport.[1] Their route of march was in plain view of Maryland Heights, and the news was immediately telegraphed from there by General Tyler.

---

[1] [*Telegram.*]

MARYLAND HEIGHTS, June 24, 1863.

H. W. HALLECK, *General-in-Chief:* —

Longstreet's corps, which camped last between Berryville and Charlestown, is to-day in motion and before 6 O. C. this morning commenced crossing by the ford one mile below Shepherdstown to Sharpburg.

GEN. TYLER, *Brigadier-General.*

This set the whole of Hooker's army in motion, on the morning of the 25th, for the Potomac. About the time, therefore, that Stuart's column appeared on the eastern side of Bull Run, on the morning of the 25th, Hancock broke up camp and started on the same road that Stuart intended to march. Hancock was ahead of him, and had the right of way. Gen. Longstreet had urged Stuart to go that route, for fear that if he went through the Shenandoah Valley, the plans of the commanding general would be disclosed to the enemy.

I am unable to understand why he could not foresee that the march of all the Confederate infantry in full view of the enemy would have the same effect. If the corps of Longstreet and Hill had delayed a single day in leaving Berryville, Stuart would have landed on the north bank of the Potomac on the night of the 25th. Hooker would then have been utterly confounded. Before he could have made up his mind what to do, the Confederate cavalry would have been watering their horses in the Susquehanna, and all the communications between Washington and the North would have been broken. But now to return to the cavalry which Stuart, under Gen. Lee's orders, had left in front of the enemy in Virginia, as he says, "*to observe his movements, and follow him in case of withdrawal.*" Of course, this duty could not be discharged without keeping in

sight of the enemy.   But instead of following, they
fell back in an opposite direction, and gave no information to Gen. Lee and no trouble to the enemy.
Gen. Lee says that on the night of the 28th he
heard through a scout that had come in that Hooker
was over the river, and was moving north.   He is
mistaken as to the date, as there is a letter of his
to Gen. Ewell, dated Chambersburg, June 28th,
7.30 A.M., which says, "I wrote you *last night*, stating that Gen. Hooker was reported to have crossed
the Potomac, and is advancing by way of Middle-
town, — the head of his column being at that point
in Frederick County, Md."   He directs Ewell to
move to Gettysburg, which had become to him what
Quatre Bras was to Wellington, when he learned
that Napoleon was over the Sombre.   In his report
of the campaign, Gen. Lee says that as soon as it
was known that the enemy had crossed into Maryland, orders were sent to Gen. Robertson to rejoin
the army "*without delay.*"   The very fact that Gen.
Lee had to send back for this cavalry shows that
it was in the wrong place, and where he did not intend it to be.   In his instructions to Stuart, when
leaving, he had said : "*Give instructions to the com-*
mander of the brigades left behind, to watch the flank
and rear of the army, and (in event of the enemy leav-
ing their front) retire from the mountains west of the
Shenandoah, leaving sufficient pickets to guard the

passes, bringing everything clean along the valley, close upon the rear of the army." It is clear that the instructions to Gen. Robertson were to leave Virginia when the enemy left; for how could he otherwise "*watch the flank and rear*" of the Confederate army, and be "*close upon*" it. Gen. Robertson [1] says that during the time he was lying in the gaps of the Virginia mountains, after the enemy had crossed the river, he was in daily communication by couriers with Gen. Lee's headquarters. [2] Then so much the worse if he did not inform him that the enemy had disappeared from his front. The inquiry is now naturally suggested, *What did he communicate?*

---

[1] See his letter of Dec. 27, 1877, in *Phila. Times.*

[2] Stuart's report says: " I submitted to the commanding general the plan of leaving a brigade or so in my present front, and passing through Hopewell, or some other gap in the Bull Run Mountain, attain the enemy's rear, passing between his main body and Washington, cross into Maryland, joining our army north of the Potomac. The commanding general wrote to me, authorizing this move if I deemed it practicable, and also what instructions should be given the officer left in command of the two brigades left in front of the enemy. He also notified me that one column should move via Gettysburg and the other via Carlisle towards the Susquehanna, and directed me, after crossing, to proceed with all dispatch to join the right (Early) of the army in Pennsylvania.

* * * * * * * *

" Robertson's and Jones's brigades, under command of the former, were left in observation of the enemy on the usual front, *with full instructions as to following up the enemy in case of withdrawal and rejoining our main army.*" This report was read by Gen. Lee and not one word of dissent by him is endorsed on it. It bears his initials in pencil, *R. E. L.*, in his own handwriting.

Again he says, " He [Gen. Lee] was fully aware
of my position and the specific duty I was then performing." But what that specific duty was no one
knows. If Gen. Lee ordered him to remain there
unemployed, then he could blame no one but himself
for the want of cavalry, and the responsibility would
rest on him.[1] But the fact that Gen. Lee sent for
him to join the army as soon as he heard that the
enemy was advancing north, is proof that he never
intended him to stay in Virginia after they had gone.
Gen. Lee had issued orders from Chambersburg for
the concentration of his army at Gettysburg, and as
he says, sent back for Robertson's command to join
the army *without delay.* When the order was read,
Gen. Robertson marched his two brigades that night
to Berryville, which is west of the mountain, on a
route almost parallel and in an opposite direction
from Gettysburg, which is east of it. On June 30,
he continued his westerly and circuitous march to Martinsburg, and on July 1, the day of the battle, crossed

---

[1] Gen. Robertson says that when he received Gen. Lee's order he
was at Ashby's Gap in the Blue Ridge in Fauquier County. Jones's
brigade was twelve miles farther north, at Snicker's Gap in Loudoun,
and joined him at Berryville. Stuart had placed them about fifteen
miles to the front of the Gaps at Middleburg to watch the enemy.
After he left, they retired to the mountain and rendered Gen. Lee no
more service while there than if they had been west of the Mississippi.

There are reports of their operations on file from all the brigade
and regimental commanders of the cavalry in this campaign *except
Gen. Robertson,* who, at his own request, was relieved of his command
as soon as he returned to Virginia.

the Potomac at Williamsport. If he had crossed at Shepherdstown and gone to Boonesboro, he might easily have reached Gettysburg after receiving Gen. Lee's order on the morning of July 1, when it was held by Buford with only two brigades of cavalry. Gen. Meade had sent off most of his cavalry in search of Stuart. It was this diversion created by Stuart that saved Gen. Lee's communications from attack. Buford was too weak to assume the offensive. On June 24, when Gen. Lee moved with Longstreet and Hill down the Shenandoah Valley, he left Gen. Robertson's command between him and the enemy. On July 3, Gen. Robertson had so manœuvred that *Gen. Lee had got between him and the enemy.* Stuart had ridden around Gen. Hooker while Gen. Robertson rode around Gen. Lee. *Sic itur ad astra.*

Since the above was written, I have found in the archives of the war office a copy of Stuart's orders to Gen. Robertson when leaving Virginia; but he does not appear to have been in the least governed by them. They confirm all I have said as to the duty required of the cavalry that were left under his command. Through abundant caution Stuart repeated them to Gen. Jones. He was instructed to watch the enemy and report their movements through a line of relay couriers to Gen. Longstreet; and when the enemy withdrew, to harass his rear and impede his march, and follow on the right of our army. There seems to have been no effort made to execute these orders; for both Gens. Lee and Longstreet say that no intelligence having been received through the cavalry of Hooker's crossing the Potomac, it was supposed that he was still south of it; while Pleasanton says that he never had a skirmish in retiring. The fact that Pleasanton's calvary corps reached Leesburg by noon of the 26th shows that they must have left Gen. Robertson's front at Aldie early that morning. In a despatch[1] from Leesburg to Hooker's headquarters dated June 26, 12.45 P.M., he significantly says that all is *quiet* towards the Blue Ridge, and that only a few calvary videttes were seen about Middleburg, and none on the Snickersville Pike. If his flank and rear had been harassed, all would not have been *quiet*. Again, Gen. Robertson was directed to keep his command on the right of the army and in contact with the enemy when they left, in

---

[1] [*Telegram.*]

LEESBURG, [VA.], 12.45 P.M.,
June 26, 1863.

MAJOR-GEN. BUTTERFIELD,
    Headquarters, A. P.

Have just arrived. One division is covering the flank from Aldie to this place by way of Mount Gilead. Three brigades of Second division are covering the three roads from Aldie and Gum Springs. *All quiet towards the Blue Ridge. Very few cavalry pickets seen near Middleburg this morning. None in the Snicker's Gap pike.*

A. PLEASANTON,
Major-General.

order that he might keep the commanding general informed of their movements.

But when Gen. Lee had sent an order for him to come on and join the army, as there could be no reason for his remaining any longer in Virginia after the enemy had left, he actually followed on the *left* and crossed the Potomac at Williamsport. Gen. Lee's *right* flank was thus left exposed to the enemy's cavalry, but fortunately they had nearly all been sent in search of Stuart. If the pressure of the column of three thousand cavalry with two batteries under Robertson had been brought to bear on the flank of the Union army, its advance into Pennsylvania would have been less rapid, and Meade could not have spared two-thirds of his cavalry to send after Stuart to embarrass his march. If the force of cavalry which Stuart left behind him had promptly moved in obedience to his orders on the 26th to place itself in its proper position on the right of the army, then it could easily have occupied Gettysburg in advance of the enemy. It did nothing of the kind, but quietly rested three days at Ashby's Gap to learn through Gen. Lee where the enemy had gone. The professed historians of the war make no mention of these facts. *Stuart is dead:* "O! for one hour of Dundee."

HEADQUARTERS, June 22, 1863.

MAJOR-GENERAL J. E. B. STUART,
    Commanding Cavalry.

GENERAL : — I have just received your note of 7.45 this morning to General Longstreet. I judge the efforts of the enemy yesterday were to arrest our progress and ascertain our whereabouts. Perhaps he is satisfied. Do you know where he is and what he is doing? I fear he will steal a march on us and get across the Potomac before we are aware. If you find that he is moving northward, and that two brigades can guard the Blue Ridge and take care of your rear, you can move with the other three into Maryland and take position on General Ewell's right, place yourself in communication with him, guard his flank, and keep him informed of the enemy's movements, and collect all the supplies you can for the use of the army. One column of General Ewell's army will probably move towards the Susquehanna by the Emmettsburg route, another by Chambersburg. Accounts from him last night state that there was no enemy west of Fredericktown. A cavalry force (about one hundred) guarded the Monocacy Bridge, which was barricaded. You will, of course, take charge of Jenkins' brigade and give him necessary instructions. All supplies taken in Maryland must be by authorized staff-officers, for their respective departments, by no one else. They will be paid for or receipts for the same given to the owners. I will send you a general order on this subject, which I wish you to see is strictly complied with.

    I am, very respectfully, your obedient servant,

                        R. E. LEE, *General.*

HEADQUARTERS, MILLWOOD, June 22, 1863, 7 P.M.

MAJ.-GEN'L J. E. B. STUART,
    Comdg Cavalry.

GENERAL : — Gen. Lee has inclosed to me this letter for you, to be forwarded to you, provided you can be spared from my front, and provided I think that you can move across the Potomac without disclosing our plans. He speaks of your leaving via Hopewell Gap and passing by the rear of the enemy. If you can get through by that route, I think that you will be less likely to indicate what our plans are, than if you should cross by passing to our rear. I forward the letter of instructions with these suggestions.

Please advise me of the condition of affairs before you leave, and order Genl. Hampton — whom I suppose you will leave here in command — to report to me at Millwood either by letter or in person, as may be most agreeable to him.   Most respectfully,

                    J. LONGSTREET,
                            Lt.-Genl.

N. B. I think that your passage of the Potomac by our rear at the present moment will, in a measure, disclose our plans. You had better not leave us, therefore, unless you can take the proposed route in rear of the enemy.

                    J. LONGSTREET,
                            Lt.-Genl.

HEADQUARTERS, ARMY OF NORTH VIRGINIA,
June 23, 1863, 5 P.M.

MAJOR-GENERAL J. E. B. STUART,
Commanding Cavalry.

GENERAL : — Your notes of 9 and 10.30 A.M. to-day have just been received. As regards the purchase of tobacco for your men, supposing that Confederate money not be taken, I am willing for your commissaries or quartermasters to purchase this tobacco and let the men get it from them ; but I can have nothing seized by the men.

If General Hooker's army remains inactive, you can leave two brigades to watch him and withdraw with the three others ; but should he not appear to be moving northward, I think you had better withdraw this side of the mountain to-morrow night, cross at Shepherdstown next day and move over to Fredericktown.

You will, however, be able to judge whether you can pass around their army without hindrance, doing them all the damage you can, and cross the river east of the mountains. In either case, after crossing the river, you must move on and feel the right of Ewell's troops, collecting information, provisions, etc.

Give instructions to the commander of the brigades left behind, to watch the flank and rear of the army and (in event of the enemy leaving their front) retire from the mountains west of the Shenandoah, leaving sufficient pickets to guard the passes, and bringing everything clean along the Valley, closing upon the rear of the army.

As regards the movements of the two brigades of the enemy moving towards Warrenton, the commander of the brigades to be left in the mountains must do what he can to counteract them ; but I think the sooner you cross into Maryland, after to-morrow, the better.

The movements of Ewell's corps are as stated in my former letter. Hill's first division will reach the Potomac to-day, and Longstreet will follow to-morrow.

Be watchful and circumspect in all your movements.

I am, very respectfully and truly yours,

R. E. LEE,

General.

————

[*Confidential.*]

HD.QRS. CAV'Y DIV.: ARMY OF N. VA.,
June 24, 1863.

BRIG.-GEN'L B. H. ROBERTSON, *Com'dg Cavalry:*

GENERAL : — Your own and Gen'l Jones's brigades will cover the front of Ashby's and Snicker's Gaps ; yourself, as senior officer, being in command.

Your object will be to watch the enemy, deceive him as to our designs, and harass his rear if you find he is retiring. Be always on the alert, let nothing escape your observation, and miss no opportunity which offers to damage the enemy.

After the enemy has moved beyond your reach, leave sufficient pickets in the mountains, and withdraw to the west side of the Shenandoah, and place a strong and relia-ble picket to watch the enemy at Harper's Ferry, cross the Potomac, and follow the army, keeping on its right and rear.

As long as the enemy remains in your front in force, unless otherwise ordered by Gen'l R. E. Lee, Lt.-Gen'l

Longstreet, or myself, hold the gaps with a line of pickets reaching across the Shenandoah by Charlestown to the Potomac.

If, in the contingency mentioned, you withdraw, sweep the valley clear of what pertains to the army, and cross the Potomac at the different points crossed by it.

You will instruct General Jones from time to time as the movements progress or events may require, and report anything of importance to Lieut.-Gen'l Longstreet, with whose position you will communicate by relays through Charlestown.

I send instructions for Gen'l Jones which please read. Avail yourself of every means in your power to increase the efficiency of your command, and keep it up to the highest number possible. Particular attention will be paid to shoeing horses, and to marching off of the turnpikes.

In case of an advance of the enemy, you will offer such resistance as will be justifiable to check him and discover his intentions; and, if possible, you will prevent him from gaining possession of the gaps.

In case of a move by the enemy upon Warrenton, you will counteract it as much as you can compatible with previous instructions.

You will have with the two brigades two batteries of horse artillery.

Very respectfully your obl. servt.

J. E. B. STUART,
Major Gen'l Com'dg.

Do not change your present line of pickets until daylight to-morrow morning unless compelled to do so.

CHAPTER XIV.

SOON after the outbreak of war in the spring of 1861 the First Regiment of Virginia Cavalry was organized with J. E. B. Stuart as colonel. He was then just twenty-eight years of age, a native of Virginia and a graduate of West Point. As lieutenant of cavalry he had had some experience in Indian warfare in the West in which he had been wounded ; and in the raid of John Brown on the United States arsenal at Harper's Ferry had acted as aide to Colonel (afterwards General) Robert E. Lee.

The First Virginia Cavalry was attached to the command of General Joseph E. Johnston in the Shenandoah valley and assigned to the duty of watching Patterson, who had crossed the Potomac and was threatening the Southern army, then at Winchester. I was a private in a company of cavalry called the Washington Mounted Rifles, which was commanded by Capt. William E. Jones, an officer who some years before had retired from the United States army, and gave the company the name of his old regiment. Jones was a graduate of West Point and had been a comrade of Stonewall

Jackson's while there. He has often entertained me in his tent at night with anecdotes of that eccentric genius. No man in the South was better qualified to mould the wild element he controlled into soldiers. His authority was exercised mildly but firmly, and to the lessons of duty and obedience he taught me I acknowledge that I am largely indebted for whatever success I may afterwards have had as a commander.

I first saw Stuart in the month of July, 1861, at a village called Bunker Hill on the pike leading from Winchester to Martinsburg, where Patterson was camped. His regiment was stationed there to observe the movements of the Union army. His personal appearance bore the stamp of his military character, the fire, the dash, the energy and physical endurance that seemed able to defy all natural laws. Simultaneously with the movement of McDowell against Beauregard, began Patterson's demonstration to keep Johnston at Winchester. It was, however, too feeble to have any effect except to neutralize his own forces. The plan of the Southern generals was to avoid a battle in the valley and concentrate their armies at Manassas. The duty was assigned to Stuart's cavalry of masking the march of Johnston to Manassas and at the same time watching Patterson. General Scott had ordered him to feel the enemy strongly and not to allow him to escape to Manassas to reinforce Beauregard. Patterson replied in the most confident tone that he was holding Johnston.

After the battle had been won by the Confederates, in reply to Scott's criticism upon him for not having engaged them, Patterson comforted him with the assurance that if he had done so, Scott would have had to mourn the defeat of two armies instead of one. The records show that at that time Patterson had about 18,000 men and Johnston about 10,000.

On the 15th of July, Patterson advanced and drove us with artillery from our camp at Bunker Hill. Stuart had none to reply with. All of us thought a battle at Winchester was imminent. Patterson had one regiment of the regular besides some volunteer cavalry from Philadelphia, but made no use of them. He never sent his cavalry outside his infantry lines, and their only service was to add to the pomp and circumstance of war on reviews and parades. He stayed one day at Bunker Hill, and then, thinking he had done enough in driving us away, turned off squarely to the left and marched down to Charlestown. He had not been in twelve miles of our army, and this was the way he executed General Scott's order to feel it strongly.

Stuart still hung so close on his flanks that he occasionally let a shell drop among us. As soon as

the movement to Charlestown was developed, Johnston received intelligence of it through Stuart.   He
saw then that Patterson did not intend an attack,
and got ready to join Beauregard.   The Union general went into camp at Charlestown while the Confederate folded his tent like the Arab and quietly
stole away.   Stuart spread a curtain of cavalry between the opposing armies which so effectually concealed the movement of Johnston, that Patterson
never suspected it until it had been accomplished.
The telegraphic correspondence at that time between Generals Scott and Patterson now reads like
an extract from the transactions of the Pickwick
Club.

On July 13th, Scott telegraphs to Patterson :
'' Make demonstrations to detain Johnston in the
valley.''   July 14th, Patterson replies : '' Will advance to-morrow.   Unless I can rout shall be care-
ful not to set him in full retreat toward Strasburg.''
He seemed to be afraid of frightening Johnston so
much that he would run away.   Again, Scott telegraphs to Patterson : '' Do not let the enemy amuse
and delay you with a small force in front whilst he
reinforces the junction with his main body.''   This
shows that General Scott, who was in Washington,
had the sagacity to discern what we were likely to
do.

On July 18th, General Scott says to him : '' **I**

have been certainly expecting you to beat the enemy. If not, to hear that you had felt him strongly, or, at least, had occupied him by threats and demonstrations." At that time Patterson was twenty miles distant from Johnston and never got any closer. This was all the feeling he did. On the same day Patterson replies : " The enemy has stolen no march on me. I have kept him actively employed, and by threats and reconnoissances in force caused him to be reinforced." At that time, Johnston was marching to Manassas, and Stuart's cavalry were watching the smoke as it curled from the Union camps at Charlestown.

Again, on July 18th, in order to make General Scott feel perfectly secure, Patterson tells him : " I have succeeded, in accordance with the wishes of the General-in-Chief, in keeping Johnston's force at Winchester. A reconnoissance in force on Tuesday caused him to be largely reinforced from Strasburg." And on July 21st, when the junction of the two armies had been effected, and the great battle was raging at Manassas, he telegraphs to Scott : " Johnston left Millwood yesterday to operate on McDowell's right and to turn through Loudoun on me."

As Patterson was haunted by the idea that Johnston was after him, although he had marched in an opposite direction, he concluded to retreat to Harper's **Ferry.** The success of Johnston's strategy in eluding Patterson and cheating him into the belief that he was still in the valley, is due to the vigilance of Stuart and his activity and skill in the management of cavalry. The Northern General never discovered how badly he had been fooled until the day of the battle, when he was too far away to give any assistance. But Stuart was not satisfied with the work he had done. After the infantry had been transferred to the railroad east of the Blue Ridge, he left a single company as a veil in front of Patterson and joined the army at Manassas on the evening before the battle. We had been almost continuously in the saddle for a week, and I have a vivid remembrance of the faces of the men—bronzed with sun and dust from the long march. The two armies were in such close contact that all knew there would be a battle on the morrow. Patterson was safe in the valley.

When he was before the committee on the Conduct of the War to give his reasons for not advancing on Johnston at Winchester, he filed a paper containing the following statement : " Among the regiments there was one of Kentucky riflemen armed with heavy bowie knives ; they refused to take more than one round of cartridges. They proposed to place themselves in the bushes for assault." Of course, no prudent commander would lead men where they would be disembowelled by an enemy hidden in the bushes. Perhaps General Patterson was imitating the example of Othello, and trying to captivate Congressmen, as the Moor did the ear of Desdemona, with tales of

> The cannibals that do each other eat ;
> The anthropophagi, and men whose heads
> Do grow beneath their shoulders.

On the night before the battle, the raw troops were excited by every noise, and the picket firing was incessant. We slept soundly in our bivouac in the pines, and early in the morning were awakened by the reveille that called us to arms. As the sun rose, the rattle of musketry began along Bull Run, and soon from one end of the line to the other there was a continuous roar of small arms and artillery.

War loses a great deal of its romance after a soldier has seen his first battle. I have a more vivid recollection of the first than the last one I was in. It is a classical maxim that it is sweet and becoming to die for one's country ; but whoever has seen the horrors of a battle-field feels that it is far sweeter to live for it. The Confederate generals had expected a battle on our right ; as a fact, our left wing was turned, and the battle was mostly fought by Johnston's troops, who, having come up the day before, had been held in reserve. Stuart's regiment having just arrived, had not been sent on the outposts, and hence is in no way responsible for the surprise. In the crisis of the battle, when Jackson with his brigade was standing like a stone wall against the advancing host, he called for Stuart's cavalry to support him. Stuart sent one squadron to Jackson's right, under the Major, who did nothing (I was with him), while with six companies he came up on Jackson's left, just in time to charge and rout the Ellsworth Zouaves. Their general, in his report, says that he was never able to rally them during the fight.

This cavalry charge had an important effect upon the fortunes of the day, as it delayed the enemy, and gave time for troops to come to the relief of Jackson, who was then hard pressed by superior numbers. Stuart afterward, with a battery of artillery, led the turning movement that caused the rout, and associated the stream of Bull Run with the most memorable panic in history. Shortly after the battle, all the cavalry of the army was organized into a brigade, with Stuart in command. Jones was also promoted to be colonel of the regiment, and Fitz Lee became lieutenant-colonel. From this time until the army evacuated Manassas, in the spring of 1862, the cavalry was almost exclusively engaged in outpost duty. McClellan kept close to the fortifications around Washington while he was organizing the army of the Potomac, and his cavalry rarely ventured beyond his infantry pickets. No field was open for brilliant exploits ; but the discipline and experience of a life on the outpost soon converted the Confederate volunteers into veterans.

Without intending any disparagement, I may say that the habits and education of Northern men had not been such as to adapt them readily to the cavalry service, without a process of drilling ; while, on the contrary, the Southern youth, who, like the ancient Persians, had been taught from his cradle " to ride, to shoot, and speak the truth," leaped into his saddle, almost a cavalryman from his birth. The Cossacks, who came from their native wilds on the Don to break the power of Napoleon, had no other training in war than the habits of nomadic life ; and in the same school were bred the Parthian horsemen who drove to despair the legions of Crassus and Antony.

I must also say that the Confederate authorities made but slight use of the advantage they enjoyed in the early periods of the war, for creating a fine body of cavalry ; and that little wisdom was shown in the use of what they did have. It would have been far better military policy, during the first winter of the war, to have saved the cavalry as McClellan did, either to lead the advance or cover the retreat in the spring campaign. It was largely consumed in work which the infantry might have done, without imposing much additional hardships on them, as the proportion of cavalry was so small. When the Southern army retired, in March, 1862, three-fourths of the horses had been broken down by the hard work of the winter, and the men had been furloughed to go home for fresh ones. The Confederate government did not furnish horses for the cavalry, but paid the men forty cents a day for the use of them. This vicious policy was the source of continual depletion of the cavalry. Stuart's old regiment,—the First Virginia Cavalry,—of which I was adjutant, with at least 800 men on its muster-rolls, did not have 150 for duty on the morning we broke up winter quarters on Bull Run. If the cavalry brigade had been cantoned on the border, in the rich counties of Fauquier and Loudoun, the ranks would have been full, and their granaries would not have been left as forage for the enemy. The Confederate army fell back leisurely from the front of Washington, and rested some weeks on the Rappahannock, waiting the development of McClellan's plans. Stuart's cavalry was the rear-guard Sumner pushed forward with a division along the Orange and Alexandria railroad, to make a demonstration and cover McClellan's operations in another direction. He rather overdid the thing. On reaching our picket line on Cedar Run, he made a grand display by deploying his whole force in an open field. I happened to be on the picket line that day, and told Col. Jones that it was only a feint to deceive us. We retired, and the enemy occupied our camping-ground that night.

The next morning Stuart was at Bealeton station ; and our skirmishers were engaged with the enemy, who was advancing towards the Rappahannock. My own regiment had just taken position on the railroad, when I rode up to Stuart, with whom I had become pretty well acquainted. Since we had left the line of Bull Run, I had several times returned on scouts for him. He said to me, " I want to find out whether this is McClellan's army or only a feint." I replied, " I will go and find out for you." I immediately started towards the rear of the enemy's column with two or three men, and reached a point some distance behind it about the time they were shelling our cavalry they had driven over the river. I saw that the enemy was only making a demonstration, and rode nearly all night to get back to Stuart. When I got to the river, we came very near being shot by our own pickets, who mistook us for the enemy. I found Stuart with Gen. Ewell, anxiously waiting to hear from me, or for the enemy to cross the river.

I have not been so fortunate as to have a poet to do for me on this occasion what Longfellow did for the midnight ride of Paul Revere. There was a drizzling rain and a dense fog ; it was impossible to see what the enemy were doing. I remember Stuart's joy and surprise when I told him that they were falling back from the river. In the rapture of the moment he told me that I could get any reward I wanted for what I had done. The only reward I asked was the opportunity to do the same thing again.[1] In ten minutes the cavalry had crossed the river and was capturing prisoners. Nothing had been left before us but a screen of cavalry, which was quickly brushed away. It now became evident that McClellan would move down the Potomac and operate against Richmond from a new base and on another line. This was the first cavalry reconnoissance that had ever been made to the rear of the enemy, and was considered as something remarkable at that time ; at a later period they were very common. Soon after this, Stuart's cavalry was transferred from the line of the Rappahannock with the rest of Johnston's army, to confront McClellan on the Peninsula. I dined with Gen. Lee at his headquarters, near Petersburg, about six weeks before the surrender. He told me then that he had been opposed to Gen. Johnston's withdrawing to the Peninsula, and had written to him while he was on the Rapidan, advising him to move back towards

---

[1] See Stuart's report to Gen. Johnston.

the Potomac. He thought that if he had done this, McClellan would have been recalled to the defence of Washington. He further said that, instead of falling back from Yorktown to Richmond, Gen. Johnston should have made a stand with his whole army, instead of a part of it, on the narrow isthmus at Williamsburg.

Just before we reached Williamsburg, news came of the passage of the conscription law, which preserved all the regimental organizations as they were. The men were held in the ranks, but allowed to elect their company officers ; and these in turn elected field officers. It is hard to reconcile democracy with military principles ; and, consequently, many of the best officers were dropped. Such was the fate of my colonel. The staff officers, not being elected, were supposed to hold over without reappointment. I immediately handed my resignation as adjutant to the new colonel,—Fitz Lee,—*who accepted it.*

The conscription law at first produced some dissatisfaction among the men, as most of them had served twelve months without a furlough ; but this soon subsided. All acquiesced in what was regarded as imperious necessity. The loss of our positions in the First Virginia Cavalry resulted in a benefit both to Jones and myself. Through the influence of Stonewall Jackson, Jones was made a brigadier-general, and soon after the death of Ashby was given the command of his brigade. Stuart invited me to come to his headquarters and act as a scout for him. In this way I began my career as a partisan, which now, when I recall it through the mist of years, seems as unreal as the lives of the Paladins.

I wish it to be understood that a scout is not a spy who goes in disguise, but a soldier in arms and uniform who reconnoitres either inside or outside an enemy's line. Such a life is full of adventure, excitement, and romance. Stuart was not only an educated, but a heaven-born soldier, whose natural genius had not been stifled by red tape and the narrow rules of the schools.

The history of the war furnishes no better type of the American soldier ; as a chief of cavalry he is without a peer. He cared little for formulas, and knew when to follow and when to disregard precedents. He was the first to see that the European methods of employing cavalry were not adapted to the conditions of modern war.[1] His inventive genius discovered new ways of making cavalry useful, that had never been dreamed of by the regular professors of the science. I will now give some illustrations of his originality and the fertility of his

---

[1] That infantry armed with repeating rifles and fixed ammunition would have destroyed the squadrons of Murat at Eylou and Mount Tabor before they ever got close enough to use their sabres.

resources. When McClellan was lying in the
swamps of the Chickahominy, the infantry lines of
the two armies were so close together that cavalry
operations in their front were impracticable. One
morning, when Stuart's headquarters were near
Richmond, he invited me to breakfast with him,
and at the table asked me to take two or three men
and find out whether McClellan was fortifying on
the Totopotomoy Creek. I had been inactive for
some time, and this was just the opportunity I
wanted. I started, but was diverted from the route
I had been directed to go by there being a flag of
truce on the road. I did not want to return without accomplishing something, so I turned north and
made a wide detour by Hanover Court House.
Although I was then engaged in the business of
breaking idols, I had not lost all reverence for
antiquity. I stopped a while to muse in the old
brick building where Patrick Henry made his first
speech at the bar, and pleaded the cause of the
people against the parsons. In order to understand
the enterprise on which I was going, a geographical
description of the country and situation of the
armies is necessary. The battle of Fair Oaks or
Seven Pines had been fought, and the army of the
Potomac was lying on the Peninsula between the
James and Pamunkey rivers, and astraddle of the
Chickahominy, which meanders between them and

finally empties into the James. McClellan's right
wing rested on the Pamunkey, with his base at the
White House and his line of supply by the York
River Railroad. His left extended to within a few
miles of the James. The Totopotomoy Creek flows
into the Pamunkey. I got down in the enemy's
lines on the Totopotomoy and ascertained that six
or eight miles of McClellan's front was a mere
shroud of cavalry pickets that covered his line of
communication with his depot at the White House.
Of course, as he had no infantry on his right there
would be no fortifications there. The idea immediately occurred to me that here was a grand opportunity for Stuart to strike a blow. It is now clear
why General Lee wanted to get information about
the enemy's fortifying the Totopotomoy.

About three weeks after that he called Jackson
from the valley, who struck McClellan on this very
ground. I was chased away from there and came
out just behind a regiment of Union cavalry going
on a scout. They very little thought that I was
coming back so soon. I hastened to Stuart's headquarters to give him the information. Everybody
there was in high glee. News had just come of
Jackson's victories over Fremont and Shields :
Cross Keyes and Port Republic had been inscribed
on his banners. It was a hot day in June, and
Stuart was sitting under the shade of a tree, and I

lay down on the grass to tell him what I had learned.
After giving him the information, I remarked, that
as the cavalry was idle, he could find on the Pamunkey something for them to do. A blow on this
weak point would greatly alarm McClellan for the
safety of his supplies, and compel him to detach
heavily from his front to guard them. After I got
through, he said to me, "Write down what you
have told me." I went to his adjutant's office and
wrote it down hurriedly ; but, not attaching much
importance to it, did not sign the writing. When
I brought the paper to Stuart he had his horse
ready to mount. He called my attention to the
omission, and I went back and signed it. He
started off at a gallop with a single courier to General Lee's headquarters. He returned that afternoon, and orders were immediately issued for a part
of the cavalry to get ready to march.

General Lee's instructions to Stuart, directing, or
rather authorizing, the expedition, are dated June
11, which shows how soon he started after my return, which was on the 10th.[1] With about 1200

---

[1] Von Borcke, a Prussian on Stuart's staff, in his "Memoirs,"
says that he and Stuart rode alone at night five miles, inside the
enemy's lines on the Chickahominy, to the house of an Irishman,
which Stuart had appointed as a rendezvous to meet a spy. The
spy not appearing, he says that he and Stuart waited for him till
daylight, and then rode to his house, just as the reveille sounded
in the Yankee camps, only 400 paces distant. Such rides, he says,

cavalry and two pieces of artillery, on the morning of June 12, Stuart left Richmond, moving in a northerly direction, to create the impression that he was going to reinforce Jackson. That night we bivouacked within a few miles of Hanover Court House. During his absence his adjutant was left in charge of his headquarters. I was present when he started. The adjutant asked him how long he would be gone. Stuart's answer was, "It may be for years, and it may be forever." Taking leave of his staff had suggested the parting from Erin and Kathleen Mavourneen.

There were many surmises as to his destination ; but I never doubted for a moment where we were going. Early the next morning Stuart sent me on in advance with a few men to Hanover Court House, and I then saw that my idea of a raid on

---

were habitual with Stuart, and, of course, Von Borcke always went with him. He adds : "The object of this excursion soon appeared. Our cavalry force received orders to provide themselves with rations for three days, and on the 12th we commenced that ride round the army of McClellan which attracted so much attention even in Europe." The Baron Munchausen, who was a countryman of Von Borcke's, never invented a purer fiction. Tradition says that King Alfred went, disguised as a harper, into the court of the Danes ; he was, however, acting as a spy, and did not go to meet one. There is not a soldier of the army of Northern Virginia who does not know that neither Stuart nor any other Confederate general ever did such a thing. Stuart employed scouts and spies to get information for him ; but they reported to him at his headquarters ; he never went either inside or outside the enemy's lines to meet them.

McClellan's lines was about to be realized. When we got within a few hundred yards of the village, a squadron of cavalry was discovered there, and I sent a man back to inform Stuart of it, so that he might send a regiment round to cut off their retreat. He ordered the First Virginia Cavalry to go ; but the enemy, suspecting that there was a stronger force than they could see, withdrew too soon to be caught.

The column then pushed rapidly towards the camp of Union cavalry at Old Church. At that place Captain Royall was stationed with two squadrons of the 5th U. S. regular cavalry. There was a running fight of several miles with the pickets, and finally we met Captain Royall, who came out with his whole command to reinforce the outpost. He had no suspicion of the number he was attacking, and as soon as he came in sight, Stuart ordered the front squadron of the 9th Virginia cavalry to charge. Royall was wounded and routed. On our side, Captain Latane was killed. We could not stay to give him even the hasty burial that the hero received who died on the ramparts of Corunna. This was left for female hands to do. The scene has been preserved on canvas by a Virginia artist. As Royall's command had been scattered, we soon had possession of his camp, and were feasting on the good things we found in it. Nearly everybody

forgot—many never knew—the danger we were in.
A mile or so on our left was an impassable river—
not more than six miles to the right were McClellan's headquarters, with Fitz John Porter's corps
and the reserve division of cavalry camped near us.
Here was the turning-point of the expedition.
Stuart was as jolly as anybody ; but his head was
always level in critical moments—even in the midst
of fun.   There was a short conference between him
and the Lees, who were the colonels of the two
Virginia regiments.   I was sitting on my horse,
buckling on a pistol I had just captured, within a
few feet of them and heard all that passed.   Stuart
was for pushing on to the York River Railroad,
which was still nine miles off.   Lee, of the 9th (son
of General R. E. Lee), was in favor of it, but Fitz
Lee was opposed.   Stuart had no idea of turning
back, and determined to go on and strike McClellan
in his rear.   In the conception and execution of
this bold enterprise he showed the genius and the
intrepid spirit that took the plunge of the Rubicon.

Just as he gave the command, " Forward !" he
turned to me, and said, " Mosby, I want you to
ride some distance ahead."   I replied :   " Very
well.   But you must give me a guide ; I don't
know the road."   He then ordered two cavalrymen
who were familiar with the country to go with me ;
and I started on towards Tunstall's station.   I was

on a slow horse ; and I remember that I had not gone very far before Stuart sent one of his staff to tell me to go faster and increase the distance between us. It was important that we should reach the railroad before dark, or reinforcements could be sent there. So I went on with my two men at a trot.[1]

Stuart's biographer, without so intending, has made a statement which if true would rob him of all the glory of the enterprise. He says that after reaching Old Church, Stuart kept on because it was safer than to go back by the route he had come. The road to Hanover Court House was open ; and it would not have been possible for the enemy to have closed it against him for several hours. The fight with Royall was near his camp, and did not last five minutes ; it took only a few minutes to destroy it. If he had intended to return by Hanover, he would have left pickets behind him to keep the way open. But he did nothing of the kind. He took no more account of his rear than Cortez did when he burned his ships, and marched to the capital of the Aztec kings. The route of the two

---

[1] Stuart's report contained recommendations of a number who had been with him for promotion. He said : " Captains W. D. Farley and J. S. Mosby, without commission, have established a claim for position which a grateful country will not, I trust, disregard. Their distinguished services run far back towards the beginning of the war, and present a shining record of daring and usefulness."

squadrons of cavalry was, in itself, an insignificant result as compared with the magnitude of the preparation. At this point, he had simply broken through McClellan's picket line, but had not gained his rear. To have returned after doing this and no more, would have been very much like the labor of a mountain and the birth of a mouse. The fight and capture of Royall's camp at Old Church occurred about two o'clock P.M., on June 13. The nearest camps were three or four miles off. Major Williams reports that he came on the ground with 380 of the 6th cavalry at 3.30 P.M., about one hour after the rear of Stuart's cavalry had passed on towards Tunstall's. This one hour would of itself have been amply sufficient to allow Stuart's return unmolested before the arrival of that force. It will hardly be contended that 380 men of any cavalry the world ever saw could have stopped Stuart with 1200 men and two pieces of artillery. The 5th U. S. cavalry came on the ground about five o'clock ; and Gen. Cook (who was Stuart's father-in-law), with the rest of his cavalry division, Warren's brigade of infantry, and a battery of artillery, reached there after dark. It is very difficult, therefore, to see what there was to prevent Stuart from returning if he had so desired. In all, there were two brigades of cavalry, one of infantry, and a battery of artillery sent in pursuit of him.

Gen. Emory, who led the advance, says that he followed on Stuart's track, and reached Tunstall's at two o'clock that night, where he found Gen. Reynolds, who had come up with a brigade of infantry on the cars about twelve o'clock. Reynolds says that our rear guard had left there about two hours before he arrived. At Tunstall's, Gen. Emory says he lost Stuart's trail, and set every squadron he had to hunting for it, and did not succeed in finding it until eight o'clock the next morning. As Stuart had left Tunstall's on the plain country road on which he had been marching all day, and on which Gen. Emory had followed him, it seems strange that 1200 cavalry, with two pieces of artillery, should have left no track behind them. Gen. Warren says that " *the moon was shining brightly, making any kind of movement for ourselves or the enemy as easy as in daylight.*"

General Cook, with the rest of the cavalry, and infantry, and artillery, arrived about 9 o'clock the next morning. General Emory then moved forward in pursuit with infantry, cavalry, and artillery. Warren says : "*It was impossible for the infantry to overtake him* [*Stuart*], *and as the cavalry did not move without us, it was impossible for them to overtake him.*" And Fitz John Porter regrets, "*That when General Cook did pursue he should have tied his legs with the infantry command.*" Perhaps General

Cook was acting on the maxim that recommends us to build a bridge of gold for a retreating foe. But then it can hardly be said that Stuart was retreating. As there were six cavalry regiments—including all the regulars—on our track, with a battery of artillery, it is hard to see the use they had for infantry, except as a brake to keep them from going too fast. The pursuit was from beginning to end a comedy of errors. The infantry could not have expected to overtake us, whereas, if we had attempted to return by the same route we came, then they might have intercepted us by remaining where they were.

Stuart was reduced to the alternative of returning home by the road along the Pamunkey, or the one up James River. If he took the latter, then a slight extension of McClellan's left flank would have barred his way. It could hardly have been imagined that we were going down to capture Fort Monroe, or that Stuart's cavalry were amphibious animals that could cross the York and James rivers without pontoons. Only the cavalry on McClellan's right was in the pursuit. He had an abundance on his left to block our way, and they had twenty-four hours' notice of our coming. Now to return to my narrative of Stuart's march. As I was jogging along with my two companions, a mile or two ahead of the column, I came upon a well-filled

sutler's wagon at a cross-roads, of which I took possession by right of discovery. At the same time,
about a mile off to my left, I could see the masts
of several vessels riding at anchor in the river. I
sent one of the men back to tell Stuart to hurry on.
The sutler was too rich a prize to abandon, so I left
the other man in charge of him and his wagon and
hurried on. Just as I turned a bend of the road, I
came plump upon another sutler, and a cavalry
vidette was by him. They were so shocked by the
apparition that they surrendered as quietly as the
coon did to Captain Scott. Tunstall's Station was
now in full view a half a mile off. I was all alone.
Just then a bugle sounded. I saw about a squadron
of cavalry drawn up in line, near the railroad.[1] I
knew that the head of our column must be close by,
and my horse was too tired to run, so I just drew
my sabre and waved it in the air. They knew from
this that support was near me. In a few seconds
our advance guard under Lieutenant Robbins appeared in sight, and the squadron in front of me
vanished from view. Robbins captured the depot
with the guard without firing a shot. Stuart soon
rode up. Just then a train of cars came in sight,
and as we had no implements with which to pull up
a rail, a number of logs were put on the track.

---

[1] 11th Pennsylvania.

When the engineer got near us, he saw that he was in a hornet's nest, and with a full head of steam dashed on under a heavy fire, knocked the logs off the track, and carried the news to the White House below. General Ingalls, who was in command of the depot there, says that he had received a telegram from General McClellan's headquarters, telling him of the attack on Royall's camp and warning him of danger. As soon then as the telegraph line was broken, which was about sunset on the 13th, it was notice to McClellan that we were in his rear and on his line of communication.

There was now but one route by which we could return, and that was up James River. Yet he made no signs of a movement to prevent it, and the only evidence that he knew of our presence is a telegram to Stanton on the next day—dated 11 A.M., June 14th, saying that a body of cavalry had passed around his right and that he had sent cavalry in pursuit to punish them. Before reaching Tunstall's, Stuart sent a squadron to burn the transports in the river and a wagon train that was loading from them. The small guard fled at the approach of our cavalry, while the schooners and wagons disappeared in smoke. As some evidence of the consternation produced by this sudden irruption, I will mention the fact, that after we left Old Church, a sergeant with twenty-five men of the

United States regular cavalry followed on under a flag of truce and surrendered to our *rear-guard*. They supposed they were cut off and surrounded. The Jeff Davis legion was the rear-guard, and these were the only enemies they saw.

The despatch to Stanton shows the bewildered state of McClellan's mind. At the time he was writing it we were lying on the banks of the Chickahominy, building a bridge to cross on. To have caught us, it was not necessary to pursue at all ; all that he had to do was to spread his wings. We halted at Tunstall's long enough for the column to close up. Our march was slow, the artillery horses had broken down, and we were encumbered with a large number of prisoners on foot, and of course we could march no faster than they did. After dark the column moved down through New Kent towards the Chickahominy. On the road were large encampments of army wagons. Many a sutler was ruined that night ; with sad hearts they fell into line with the prisoners, and saw their wagons, with their contents, vanish in flames. The heavens were lurid with the light reflected from the burning trains, and our track was as brilliant as the tail of a comet.

The Count of Paris, who was on McClellan's staff, thus describes Stuart's march : " But night had come, and the fires kindled by his hand flashing above the forest were so many signals which drew the Federals on his track." Now, the Count of Paris evidently means that the glowing sky ought to have been a guide to the Federal generals as the pillar of fire was to Moses. As a fact, the only pursuers we saw were those who came after us to surrender under a flag of truce. Stuart halted three hours at Baltimore Store, only five miles from Tunstall's. At twelve o'clock he started again for a ford of the Chickahominy, which was eight miles distant, and reached it about daylight.

That summer night was a carnival of fun I can never forget. Nobody thought of danger or of sleep, when champagne bottles were bursting, and Rhine wine was flowing in copious streams. All had perfect confidence in their leader. In the riot among the sutlers' stores "grim-visaged war had smoothed his wrinkled front," and Mars resigned his sceptre to the jolly god. The discipline of soldiers for a while gave way to the wild revelry of the crew of Comus. During all of this time General Emory was a few miles off, at Tunstall's Station, hunting our tracks in the sand with a lighted candle. Stuart had expected to ford the Chickahominy ; but when we got there, it was found overflowing from the recent rains, and impassable. Up to this point our progress had been as easy as the descent to Avernus ; but now, to get over the river, *hic labor,*

hic opus est. He was fortunate in having two
guides, Christian and Frayser, who lived in the
neighborhood, and knew all the roads and fords on
the river. Christian knew of a bridge, or rather,
where a bridge had been, about a mile below the
ford, and the column was immediately headed for
it. But it had been destroyed, and nothing was
left but some of the piles standing in the water.
He was again fortunate in having two men, Burke
and Hagan, who knew something about bridge-
building. Near by were the remains of an old ware-
house, out of which they built a bridge. It was
marvellous with what rapidity the structure grew ;
in a few hours it was finished—it seemed almost by
magic. It was not as good a bridge as Cæsar threw
over the Rhine, but it was good enough for our
purpose. While the men were at work upon it,
Stuart was lying down on the bank of the stream,
in the gayest humor I ever saw him, laughing at the
prank he had played on McClellan.

As I was a believer in the Napoleonic maxim of
making war support war, I had foraged extensively
during the night, and from the sutlers' stores
spread a feast that Epicurus might have envied.
During all the long hours that we lay on the bank
of the river waiting for the bridge, no enemy appeared in sight. That was a mystery nobody could
understand. There was some apprehension that

McClellan was allowing us to cross over in order to entrap us in the forks of the Chickahominy. When, at last, about two o'clock, the cavalry, artillery, prisoners and captured horses and mules were all over, and fire had been set to the bridge, some of Rush's lancers came on a hill and took a farewell look at us. They came, and saw, and went away, taking as their only trophy a drunken Dutchman we had left on the road. General Emory received news of the crossing eight miles off at Baltimore Store. Our escape over the river was immediately reported to him. In his official report, he says that we crossed the Chickahominy at daylight and that we left faster than we came. Now, I am unable to see the evidence of any particular haste in the march : in fact, it seems to have been conducted very leisurely. About one o'clock P.M., on the 13th, we captured Royall's camp at Old Church ; about sunset we reached Tunstall's, nine miles distant, and at daylight on the 14th got to a point on the Chickahominy twelve miles from there, where we stayed until noon. So if we had been pursued at the rate of a mile an hour, we would have been overtaken.

But the danger was not over when we were over the Chickahominy. We were still thirty-five miles from Richmond and in the rear of McClellan's army, which was five or six miles above us. It was necessary to pass through swamps where the horses

sunk to their saddle girths, and when we emerged
from these, we had to go for twenty miles on a road
in full view of the enemy's gunboats on one side of
us in the James River, and McClellan's army within
a few miles on the other. Nothing would have
been easier than for him to have thrown a division
of infantry as well as cavalry across our path. Then
nothing could have saved us except such a miracle
as destroyed Pharaoh and his host. Stuart, appre-
hending a movement on McClellan's left, had sent
a messenger early in the morning to General Lee
requesting him to make a diversion in his favor.
But we were out of danger before he had time to
do it. After getting through the swamp the command halted in Charles City for several hours to
give rest to the men and horses. Stuart then
turned over the command to Fitz Lee, as we were
then in comparative safety, and with two men rode
on to General Lee's headquarters, which he reached
about daybreak the next morning. During the
night march I was in advance of the column, but
saw nothing in the path except occasionally a negro
who would dart across it going into the Union lines.
Early in the morning, just as I got in sight of Richmond, I met Stuart returning to the command.
Although he had been in the saddle two days and
nights without sleep, he was as gay as a lark and
showed no signs of weariness. He had a right to

be proud ; for he had performed a feat that to this day has no parallel in the annals of war. I said to him, " This will make you a major-general." He said, " No, I don't think I can be a major-general until we have 10,000 cavalry." But in six weeks he had that rank.

This expedition, in which Stuart had ridden around McClellan in a circle of a radius of ten miles, created almost as much astonishment in Richmond and even in Europe as if he had dropped from the clouds, and made him the hero of the army. It had an electric effect on the *morale* of the Confederate troops and excited their enthusiasm to a high pitch. Always after that the sight of Stuart on the field was like

> A blast of that dread horn
> On Fontarabian echoes borne.

McClellan attempts in his report to belittle it, by saying that in this affair Stuart's cavalry did nothing but gain a little *éclat ;* but with more truth it might be said that by it he lost a good deal. His staff officer, the Count of Paris, says, in reference to these operations of our cavalry : " They had, in point of fact, created a great commotion, shaken the confidence of the North in McClellan, and made the first experiment in those great cavalry expeditions which subsequently played so novel and so important a part during the war. "

At midnight, on June 14, at the very hour when we were marching along his left flank, McClellan telegraphed to Stanton, "All quiet in every direction ; the stampede of last night has passed away." In his telegram six hours before, he had said that we ran away from an infantry force, at Tunstall's, that he had sent after us. The fact was that we left that place long before the infantry arrived there, and never heard of it until long after we left. Gen. Reynolds says he never saw us. The stampede that McClellan talks about was not in *our* ranks. The Count of Paris again says : "As soon as he [Stuart] was known to be at Tunstall's, McClellan had divined his purpose, and despatched Averill to intercept him."

I have made a diligent examination of the archives of the war, but have been unable to find any authority for this statement. The despatches of the general-in-chief, the corps, division, brigade, and regimental commanders, in reference to this *raid*, have all been published, besides the report of Col. Clitz, who was ordered to investigate the conduct of those who were charged with the pursuit. They all relate to the operations on McClellan's right, and there is perfect silence as to any attempt to intercept us on his left, or any order to do so. Averill, who was stationed with the cavalry on the left flank, is nowhere mentioned, and there is no report from him.

After we crossed the Chickahominy we were in a *cul de sac*, formed by the junction of that river with the James. Yet we never saw an enemy in that vicinity, although they must or ought to have had twenty-four hours' notice that we were coming, as the army headquarters were connected with each corps by both telegraph lines and signal stations.

As McClellan was very much criticised for permitting Stuart to escape, if it had been due to the failure of Averill or any one else to execute his orders, he would have put the blame where it belonged. McClellan's conduct on this occasion has always been unaccountable to me, and the only explanation I have ever seen of it is in the report of Gen. Pleasanton, who soon after that became his chief of cavalry. Pleasanton says : " McClellan dreaded the rebel cavalry, and supposed that by placing his army on a peninsula, with a deep river on each side, he was safe from that arm of the enemy ; but the humiliation on the Chickahominy, of having a few thousand of the enemy's cavalry ride completely around his army, and the ignominious retreat to Harrison's Landing, are additional instances in support of the maxim ' that a general who disregards the rules of war finds himself overwhelmed by the consequences of such neglect, when the crisis of battle follows.' " [1]

[1] This was written by Pleasanton after the war. He does not seem to have felt the humiliation of Stuart's ride around him to

At that time Pleasanton was commanding the 2d U. S. Cavalry. The telegraph line at Tunstall's was repaired soon after Reynolds arrived, on the night of the 13th ; and it is impossible to believe that he and Ingalls did not inform the general-in-chief which way we had gone. Stuart then had no choice of routes, but was confined to the road up James River, or not to return at all. This raid is unique, and distinguished from all others on either side during the war, on account of the narrow limits in which the cavalry was compelled to operate. From the time when he broke through McClellan's line on his right until he had passed around him on his left Stuart was enclosed by three unfordable rivers, over one of which he had to build a bridge to cross. During the whole operation the cavalry never drew a sabre except at the first picket post they encountered. But it was something more than a mere raid on McClellan's communications ; it was, in fact, a *reconnoissance* in force to ascertain the exact location of the different corps of his army, and the prelude to the great battles that began ten days afterwards, in which Jackson's flank was covered by Stuart's cavalry.[1]

Chambersburg, when he, as chief of cavalry of the army of the Potomac, was charged with the duty of pursuing him.

[1] General Lee's congratulatory order is as follows :

HEADQUARTERS DEPARTMENT OF NORTHERN VA.,
General Orders, No. 74.   June 23, 1862.

The commanding general announces with great satisfaction to

The seven days' battles were fought behind in-
trenchments, and in swamps which afforded no opportunity for the use of cavalry except in guarding
the flanks of the infantry and the minor operations

---

the army the brilliant exploit of Brigadier-General J. E. B. Stuart,
with part of the troops under his command. This gallant officer,
with portions of the 1st, 4th, and 9th Virginia Cavalry, a part of
the Jeff Davis Legion, with whom were the Boykin Rangers, and
a section of the Stuart Horse Artillery, on the 13th, 14th, and 15th
of June, made a reconnoissance between the Pamunkey and the
Chickahominy rivers, and succeeded in passing around the rear of
the whole of the Union army, routing the enemy in a series of
skirmishes, taking a number of prisoners, and destroying and capturing stores to a large amount. Having most successfully accomplished its object, the expedition recrossed the Chickahominy
almost in the presence of the enemy, with the same coolness and
address that marked every step of its progress, and with the loss
of but one man, the lamented Captain Latanè, of the 9th Virginia
Cavalry, who fell bravely leading a successful charge against a
superior force of the enemy. In announcing the signal success to
the army, the general commanding takes great pleasure in express-
ing his admiration of the courage and skill so conspicuously exhibited throughout by the general and the officers and men under
his command. In addition to the officers honorably mentioned in
the report of the expedition, the conduct of the following privates
has received the special commendation of their respective commanders : Private Thomas D. Clapp, Co. D, 1st Virginia Cavalry,
and J. S. Mosby, serving in the same regiment ; privates Ashton,
Brent, R. Herring, F. Herring, and F. Coleman, Co. E, 9th Virginia Cavalry.

By command of

R. H. CHIETON, A. A. G.   GENERAL LEE.

In General McClellan's posthumous book there is a private letter
of his, dated June 15th, 10.45 P.M., in which he says : " I then
gave orders to Averill for a surprise party to-morrow, to repay
Secesh for his raid of day before yesterday." So the surprise party
was not ordered until Stuart had got back to camp.

of outpost duty. When they were over, the cavalry had a short respite from labor. I never could rest inactive ; and so I asked Stuart to let me take a party of men to northern Virginia.

Gen. Pope had then just assumed command of that department. He had a long line of communications to guard ; and his scattered army corps offered fine opportunities for partisan war. The wiser policy of concentration had not then been adopted by the Federal generals. Stuart was recruiting his cavalry, and was not willing to spare any for detached service ; but gave me a letter of introduction to Gen. Jackson, who had been sent up to Gordonsville to observe Pope. He sent him by me a copy of Napoleon's maxims, which had just been published in Richmond. Stuart wanted Jackson to furnish a detail of cavalry to go with me behind Pope, who had just published the fact to the world that he intended to leave his rear to take care of itself. With a single companion, and full of enthusiasm, I started on my mission to Jackson. I concluded to take the cars at Beaver Dam and go on in advance to his headquarters and wait there for my horse to be led on. I was sitting in the depot, and my companion had hardly got out of sight, when a regiment of Union cavalry rode up, and put an attachment upon my person. They had ridden all night from Fredericksburg to capture the train which was due in a few minutes. I was chagrined, not only at being a prisoner, but because my cherished hopes were now disappointed. The regiment fronted into a line to wait for the cars ; and they placed me in the front rank. I called to an officer, and protested against being put where I would be shot by the guard on the train. For some reason, the commanding officer gave orders to leave ; perhaps it was because he was as much opposed to being shot as I was. The train soon afterwards arrived ; and I do not think there were any soldiers on it. That night, I slept on the floor of the guard-house at Fredericksburg ; on the next day the *cartel* for the exchange of prisoners was agreed on. My imprisonment lasted ten days ; and I confess that I rather enjoyed my visit to Washington. I kept up my habits as a scout, and collected a large budget of information. The steamer on which I came back lay four days in Hampton Roads, and then proceeded up James River. When we first arrived there I noticed a large number of transports, with troops on board, lying near Newport News, and learned that they belonged to Burnside's corps just arrived from North Carolina. Here, now, was a problem for me to solve. Where were they going ? to reinforce Pope or McClellan ? I set about to find out. If they went to Pope it meant the withdrawal of McClellan. The captain of the steamer promised me to find out their destination. A few hours before we left, I observed them all coming down and passing out by Fort Monroe. When the captain returned from on shore, he told me that the transports were going up the Potomac. This settled the question ; the Peninsula campaign was over.

About ten o'clock in the morning we reached the point on James River where the commissioners had met. I knew that it would take several hours to complete the exchange and every minute then was precious. I whispered to the Confederate commissioner—Judge Culd—that I had important news for General Lee and he let me go immediately. I started off with a haversack full of lemons I had bought at Fort Monroe to walk twelve miles to headquarters on a hot day in August. I trudged on several hours weary and footsore, until completely exhausted I had fallen down on the roadside. While lying there a horseman of the Hampton Legion came riding by, and I stopped him and explained my condition and anxiety to see General Lee. He dismounted, put me on his horse, took me to his camp near by, and, getting a horse for himself, went with me to the general's headquarters. I wish that I knew his name that I might record it with the praise that is due to his generous deed. The first one I met at headquarters, with a good deal of the insolence of office, told me that I could not see the general. I tried to explain that I did not come to ask a favor, but to bring him important information. Another one of the staff standing by told me to wait a moment. He stepped into the adjoining room and soon called me in. I now found myself for the first time in the presence of the great commander of the Army of Northern Virginia. He was alone and poring over some maps on the table, and no doubt planning a new campaign. Although his manner was gentle and kind, I felt for him an awe and veneration which I have never felt for any other man. He was then the foremost man in all the world, and I almost imagined that I saw one of the Homeric heroes before me. With some embarrassment I told what I had learned about Burnside's troops. He listened attentively, and after I was through called to a staff officer to have a man ready to take a despatch to General Jackson. At that time communication was kept up between them by a line of relay couriers. They were afraid to trust the telegraph that had been tampered with by raiding parties from Fredericksburg. Jackson received the despatch that night informing him that Burnside was on his way to Pope, and hastened to strike him at Cedar Mountain before reinforcements could arrive. Pope says, " This battle was fought at a distance of more than one hundred miles from Richmond, only five days

after General McClellan received his orders to withdraw and five days before he had commenced to do
so, or had embarked a man.'' When the Army of
the Potomac was being withdrawn from the front of
Richmond, Gen. Lee began to transfer his own to
the line of the Rapidan. Stuart, with his staff,
came ahead by rail and left Fitz Lee to bring on
the cavalry division. I joined him on the evening
of August 17th, and that night we rode to a place
called Vidiersville in Orange County, where we expected to find the cavalry. It had not, however,
come up, and Stuart sent his adjutant to look for
it, and the rest of us—five in number—unsaddled
our horses and lay down to sleep on the porch of a
house by the roadside. We were outside our picket
lines and in a mile or so of the enemy on the river,
but did not think there was much risk in spending
the night there.

About sunrise the next morning a young man
named Gibson, who had been a fellow-prisoner with
me in the Old Capitol, woke me up and said that
he heard the tramp of cavalry down the road. We
saddled quickly, and started to see what it was, but
first woke Stuart up. As Fitz Lee was due, we
supposed it was our own cavalry, but there was a
chance that it might be the enemy, and we did not
want to be again caught napping. After going
about two hundred yards, we saw through the

morning mist a body of cavalry that had stopped at a house to search it. We halted, but could not tell who they were. Presently two officers rode forward and began firing on us. This convinced me that they were no friends of mine, and as neither one of us had a pistol or a sabre, I am not ashamed to say that we turned and ran away with the Yankee cavalry close after us. The firing saved Stuart. He had walked out into the yard bareheaded, and when he heard it, mounted his horse and leaped over the fence, and escaped through the back yard with one of his aides just as Gibson and I passed by at full speed. The cavalry stopped the pursuit to pick up Stuart's hat and cloak and the nice patent-leather haversack I had brought from Washington, which we had left on the porch. It was a scouting party General Pope had sent out. They had caught Stuart's adjutant during the night and found on him a letter from General Lee, disclosing the fact that he would cross the river to attack Pope on the 20th. So Pope, on the 18th, issued orders to withdraw beyond the line of the Rappahannock ; he had already received information through a spy that our whole army was assembling in his front and was about retreating anyway. If the cavalry had not stopped at the house they would have caught us all asleep.

Von Borcke, a Prussian officer on Stuart's staff,

who published a mass of fables, under the title of
" Memoirs of the Confederate War," gives an account of this affair, in which he represents himself
as playing a most heroic part. As Gibson and I
were between him and the enemy, and running with
all our might, it is hard to discover any heroism in
anybody. Von Borcke's horse ran faster than ours,
and that was the only distinction he won. The
chase was soon over, and we returned immediately
to look over the ground. Just as Stuart got in
sight of the house, he saw the enemy going off in
triumph with his hat and cloak. In two days the
armies were again confronting each other on the
Rappahannock ; on the morning of the 22d the
Confederate column began a movement up the river
to turn Pope's right. Jackson's corps was just in
rear of the cavalry. When we got to Waterloo
bridge, where we crossed, Stuart galloped by, and
said to me, laughing, as he passed, " I am going
after my hat." I had no idea then that what he
said would come true. He had heard that Pope
had his wagon trains parked at Catlett's, on the
Orange and Alexandria Railroad, and was going
after them. Pope's headquarters were ten or twelve
miles distant, at Rappahannock Station. Stuart
had with him about 1500 cavalry and two pieces of
artillery. We passed around to Pope's rear unob-
served, and got to Catlett's just after dark. A

picket post on the road was captured without any
alarm, and the guards with the trains had no suspicion of our presence until we rode into their
camp. General Pope unjustly censures them. Con-
sidering the surprise, I think they did remarkably
well. It was no fault of theirs that Stuart had got
to the rear of their army without being discovered.
It was the duty of their cavalry on the front to
watch him, and tell them he was coming. Fortunately for Pope, the most terrific storm I ever saw
came up before we reached Catlett's. But for that,
nearly the whole of the transportation of his army
would have been destroyed. The night was pitch
dark and the rain fell in torrents. Flashes of lightning would often illuminate the scene, and peals of
thunder seemed to roll from pole to pole. Stuart
halted about half a mile from the station, and sent
the First and Fifth Virginia cavalry to destroy a
large park of wagons whose camp-fires could be
seen. I went along with my old regiment. We
had to cross a railroad embankment and a ditch, of
which the men knew nothing until they tumbled
into it. Most of them scrambled out, and got into
the camp on the other side. It was defended by
the Bucktails, who, under cover of the wagons and
the darkness, poured a hot fire into us. All that
we could see was the flashes from their guns. The
animals became frightened, and increased the noise

and confusion of the fight. The shooting and shouting of the men, the braying of the mules, the glare of the lightning and roll of the thunder, made it seem like all Pandemonium had broken loose.

But cavalry, in a fight against invisible infantry, is defenceless. We left the camp with little or no damage to ourselves or the enemy. Other detachments were more successful in burning wagons and making captures. A party was sent to burn the railroad bridge over Cedar Run ; but in such a storm they might just as well have tried to burn the creek. It happened that not far from Catlett's we met a negro in the road, who recognized Stuart as an old acquaintance, and offered to conduct him to Pope's headquarter wagons. The Ninth Virginia cavalry was sent with the guide after them. A festive party of quartermasters and commissaries was captured there, together with Pope's money-chest, despatch book, and correspondence, and also his wardrobe, including *his hat* and ostrich plume. Stuart was now revenged—he had swapped hats with Pope.

The material results of the expedition were not what had been expected. The storm of that night —which caused a rise of six feet in the river—was the salvation of Pope. The *raid* had, however, a demoralizing effect on the army whose communication had been so audaciously assailed. Von Borcke, as usual, relates prodigies he performed that were never surpassed by Amadis of Gaul. He says that he was detailed by Stuart to capture Pope, and tells how he entered his tent shortly after he had left. Now Pope had never been on the spot ; his head-quarters were then fifteen miles from there ; and Stuart knew that a general commanding an army does not sleep with his wagon trains. We returned the next morning by the same route we came, but never saw an enemy. It would be a natural question to ask—what was Pope doing with his cavalry ? In the storm and darkness we had failed to cut the telegraph wire, so Pope kept up communication with Washington. At five o'clock P.M. that day— when Stuart's cavalry was in the rear and within a few miles of Catlett's, he told Halleck, "*The enemy has made no attempt to-day to cross the river.*" At nine o'clock that night, when we were plundering his headquarter trains, he tells Halleck a heavy force had crossed the river that day, and asked him to send up a brigade to guard the bridge over Cedar Run. But for the providential rain the bridge would have then been burning, and Halleck would have been saved the trouble of sending infantry to protect it. Pope had no idea where we were. Fifteen minutes later, he tells Halleck, that he must either fall back behind Cedar Run, or cross the Rappahannock at daybreak the next morning and assail the rear of the Confederate army. Halleck advised the latter movement. Pope said the rise of the river that night that swept away his bridges prevented his crossing. Here Providence stepped in again and saved him. If the " stars in their courses fought against Sisera," so did the floods against Robert E. Lee in this campaign.

At that time Jackson and Longstreet were in front of Pope, and Stuart was behind him. A week after this he was defeated, when we were no stronger and he had received at least 25,000 reinforcements from McClellan. But General Pope had left out an important factor in his calculation,—and that was Stonewall Jackson. He had already thrown one of his brigades over the river at Sulphur Springs, but the storm arrested the passage of the others. If General Pope had attempted such a movement as he indicated to Halleck, General Lee would not have interfered with it but let him go on. Jackson and Stuart would then have swept down the north bank of the river in his rear, and General Pope would have found himself in the condition of a fly in an exhausted receiver. This would have saved Jackson the long flank march he afterwards made to Manassas without involving his separation from Longstreet. Speaking of the raid on Catlett's, General Pope says : " At the time this cavalry force attacked Catlett's—and it certainly was not more than three hundred strong—our whole army trains were parked at that place, and were guarded by not less than 1500 infantry and five companies of cavalry. The success of this small party of the enemy, although very trifling and attended with but very little damage, was most *disgraceful* to the force that had been left in charge of the trains." It was certainly not the fault of the troops guarding the trains that they had no notice that we were coming ; and I think he has greatly exaggerated their number.

On the 25th, Jackson, having gone higher up the river, crossed the Rappahannock four miles above Waterloo Bridge, which was held by Sigel's Corps and Buford's Cavalry. The Black Horse Company [1] acted as his escort, and the Second Virginia Cavalry led the advance. The signal stations near the rivers reported this movement immediately to Gen. Pope. An officer in the army under Pope, who had been a classmate of Jackson's at West Point, thus speaks of the great hero and his wonderful march : " In that devotion which men yield to monarchs of the battle-field ; in that glow of pride which men share with the great chieftain whose powers have created chances and directed results,—the soldier subjects under Napoleon Bonaparte were closely allied in

---

[1] Commanded by Capt. A. D. Payne.

enthusiasm, in worship, and in admiration with the soldier citizens under Stonewall Jackson." . . .

"The sun sank down ; the stars appeared ; the night sped on till nearly twelve, when Jackson's advance had approached within one mile of Salem, where, as his weary column sank down to rest, Mc-Dowell received the message that Pope believed the enemy was marching for the *Shenandoah Valley by way of Front Royal and Luray.*"

On the mathematical principle that parallel lines meet in infinity, Jackson might have reached the valley by the route he had travelled. His camp that night was in Pope's rear, and in twelve miles of McDowell, who was occupying Warrenton. But Gen. Pope was bewildered, and appeared to have no suspicion of where he was going. At daylight no reveille sounded in the Confederate camps ; but Jackson moved silently on, and turned to the east. After his column had passed out of sight of the signal stations, Gen. Pope seemed to lose entirely the touch of it ; but the " lost Pleiad " kept on its way. A competent general would have struck Jackson's flank with a cavalry reconnoissance on his first day's march. I do not know whether the failure to do so was the fault of the chief of cavalry or the commander-in-chief.

On the 26th, before daylight, Stuart's cavalry corps crossed the Rappahannock and followed the route Jackson had taken the day before, until it got to Salem, and then turned to the right. About four o'clock P.M., we overtook Gen. Jackson at Gainesville ; having marched all day around the flank and rear of the Federal army without seeing an enemy. We were now within about seven miles of Manassas Junction. On the same day, Long-street followed on Jackson's track. While all this was going on in his rear, Gen. Pope's attention had been attracted by some Confederate batteries that kept up a fire in his front. His army remained motionless. Its very tranquillity at last became op-pressive ; some feared that it was the awful stillness that precedes the storm ; that he was imitating Napoleon at Austerlitz, and allowing one wing of our army to be extended in order to pierce its centre and destroy it. About six o'clock on the afternoon of the 26th, the advance of Jackson's column, under Col. Munford, struck the Orange & Alexandria Railroad at Bristoe Station, nine miles from Pope's headquarters, which were at Warrenton Junction. The small guard was surprised and captured ; they had no more expectation of seeing Stonewall Jack-son than Hamlet's ghost. Just then a train came up, and ran the gauntlet under fire, that carried the astounding news to Manassas, five miles off. From there it was telegraphed to Washington. Two more trains came along in a few minutes, that had just left headquarters, and were caught. Stuart was then sent on with a force of infantry and cavalry to capture Manassas, which, with all its immense stores, fell into his hands. Twenty thousand Confederate troops were now behind Gen. Pope ; and Longstreet was marching around his flank ; but his army still faced the other way. As Gen. Jackson says, " My command was now in the rear of Gen. Pope's army, separating it from the Federal capital and base of supplies."

This march of Jackson's I regard as one of the most wonderful things ever achieved in war. Gen. Pope says that it " was plainly seen and promptly reported to Gen. Halleck," but that so confidently did he rely on troops promised from Washington being in position to oppose Jackson that it gave him no uneasiness. That it gave Gen. Pope no uneasiness, I think is due to the fact that *he knew nothing about it*. It certainly would have given Napoleon or Wellington a good deal of uneasiness to have had Stonewall Jackson with 20,000 men in his rear and in nine miles of his headquarters. Now, it seems to me that his knowledge of what Jackson was doing cannot be reconciled with fidelity to his government, and his contemporaneous despatches and conduct. *They* can only be explained on the theory of his ignorance of the movement, or his *co-operation* with Jackson. The night before he had told McDowell that he believed the Confederate troops had gone to the Shenandoah valley. Jackson, I know, did marvellous things ; but Gen. Pope could hardly have thought he could march an army east and west at the same time. If he knew that Jackson was going to Manassas, he could not have believed that he had gone to the valley. Admitting that he thought Franklin's corps was at Manassas to meet him, he would be a curious commander-in-chief not to inquire if it was or not to give his subordinate warning of the enemy's approach, in order that he might get ready to fight, or burn his stores and run away. If he had even called the telegraph operators at Bristoe and Manassas, they could have told him that there were just enough troops there to get caught, and that they knew nothing of Jackson's coming. He tells McDowell, *after* Jackson got to Bristoe, that the enemy's cavalry have interrupted communication with Manassas, and orders a single regiment to go down on the cars to repair the damage. Did he think one regiment could drive Stonewall Jackson away ?

The next morning Halleck sends up a brigade to Manassas, that was almost annihilated, —its commander killed, and the train captured on which they came. If Halleck had known he was sending them into the jaws of death, he would have incurred a criminal responsibility. All of General Pope's

orders and despatches at the time have been published ; there is not a hint in any of them that he
knew of Jackson's movement around him. The
first time he suspected it was when the telegraph
wire was cut, and he had to stop talking with Halleck. Three hours after that, McDowell telegraphs
to Pope that an *intelligent* negro had just come in
and reported that Jackson had passed through
Thoroughfare Gap that day. Pope's answer shows
that this news was a revelation and a surprise to
him.

At that time Jackson's men, after a march of over
fifty miles in two days, were eating his rations in
sight of the blazing bridges and railroad trains at
Manassas. The next day a cavalry reconnoissance
under Buford was ordered to Salem, to ascertain
the truth of the negro's statement. If it had been
sent two days earlier it might have done some good.
But Pope did not wait to hear from Buford, but
changed front and hastened towards Manassas to
recover his communications. Buford returned with
his broken-down cavalry to Warrenton that night,
but Pope's whole army had gone. During that day
Jackson's wearied soldiers were resting and refresh-
ing themselves from their abundant spoils. At
night Jackson marched away towards Thoroughfare
to unite with Longstreet. The supplies that he
could not transport were burned. Pope's army

with the railroad broken was now in a starving condition.[1]   To lead Pope astray, A. P. Hill's division
was sent a roundabout way by Centreville and re-
joined Jackson the next day at Sudley.

The reason that Jackson left Manassas was that
Stuart had captured a despatch showing that Pope
was concentrating his army on that point.   General
Jackson says : " General Stuart kept me advised of
the movements of the enemy."   In a despatch to
Fitz John Porter on the evening of the 27th, Pope
ordered him to be at Bristoe at daylight the next
morning to bag Jackson who was then five miles
off.   General Pope says that Jackson made a mistake in leaving Manassas before he got there.   If
Jackson went there to be caught it was.   If Pope
had reached the place at daylight he would have
found nothing but a rear-guard of Stuart's cavalry.
He has censured Porter for not getting there in time
to bag Jackson.   Pope himself arrived about noon.
It happened that the evening before I rode off to a
farmer's house to get some supper and slept under
a tree in the yard.   The next morning I returned
to the Junction thinking our army was still there.
I found the place deserted and as silent as the cities
of the plain.   So, if General Pope and Fitz John
Porter had come at that time they might have

---

[1] See his despatch to Halleck.

caught *me*, that is, if their horses were faster than mine. Pope was deceived by Jackson's stratagem and marched off to Centreville to find him. Every step he took in that direction carried him farther from Jackson. He seemed to be groping in the dark. Instead of marching his infantry off in the morning on a fool's errand to Manassas in search of Jackson he ought first to have felt the enemy with his cavalry, and then manœuvred his army so as to intercept his junction with Longstreet. Pope did exactly the reverse.

On the evening of the 28th, Longstreet drove Ricketts' division from Thoroughfare and the head of his column bivouacked in about six miles of Jackson. During the fight I rode with Stuart towards the Gap.

As Ricketts was then between him and Longstreet, Stuart sent a despatch by a trusty messenger urging him to press on to the support of Jackson.

I do not think any other commander ever performed such a feat, or extricated himself from such perils as environed Jackson on this expedition. His success was largely due to Stuart's cavalry, who were the eyes of the army, that brought him quick intelligence of the enemy, and as the Count of Paris says, " screened all Jackson's movements as with an impenetrable veil." On the morning of the 29th, in a despatch to Porter and McDowell, Gen.

Pope says : " The indications are that the whole force of the enemy is moving in this direction at a pace that will bring them here by *to-morrow* night or *next* morning." His cavalry could not then have informed him of the result of the combat between Longstreet and Ricketts on the afternoon before ; for it was impossible for him to believe that the man who was called the war-horse of the Southern Army would take two days to march six miles with the thunders of battle rolling in his ears. General Pope does not seem to have recovered his mental equilibrium when he wrote his report, for he says, in one place, " Every indication during the night of the 29th and up to 10 o'clock on the morning of the 30th pointed to the *retreat* of the enemy from our front ;" and further on he says, " During the whole night of the 29th and the morning of the 30th the *advance* of the main army under Lee was arriving on the field to reinforce Jackson." That is, the arrival of 30,000 fresh Confederate troops on the field was a sign to Gen. Pope that they were running away.

No one can study this campaign without being struck by the marked difference between the commanders of the two armies in the employment of their cavalry. A distinguished general who served under Pope says : " That judicious use of cavalry by which Jackson covered his front, concealed his movements, discovered his enemies, and succeeded in his raids, had not at that period been generally appreciated by Federal commanders, and was almost entirely neglected by Pope."

I cannot close this account of the part borne by Stuart's cavalry in this campaign without some reference to the use that has been made of his report of it by the partisans of General Pope, and the criticism it has borne from the friends of General Porter. It is remarkable that both parties should agree in the construction put upon it, and that so clearly a wrong one. One side refers to it to prove the assertion of General Pope : " I believe—in fact I am positive—that at five o'clock on the afternoon of the 29th General Porter had in his front no considerable body of the enemy. I believed then—as I am very sure now—that it was easily practicable for him to have turned the right flank of Jackson and to have fallen on his rear : and if he had done so, we should have gained a decisive victory over the army under Jackson before he could have been joined by any of the forces of Longstreet," etc. He further says that about sunset of the 29th the advance of Longstreet began to arrive on the field. The essence of the controversy is the time of Longstreet's arrival. Could Porter have reached Gainesville, the objective point on which he and Longstreet marched that day, in time to have executed

the order of 4.30 P.M. of the 29th to turn the Confederate flank? While the order does not specify
Jackson's, but says the enemy's flank, it clearly re-
ferred to Jackson, for General Pope asserted that
Longstreet was not then on the field and could not
arrive before the next day. As Porter and Longstreet had camped the night before about the same
distance from that place, and as Porter,[1] owing to
contradictory orders, had marched twice the distance that Longstreet did, the presumption is that
the latter arrived there first.

To my mind Stuart is a conclusive witness for
Porter. Yet one critic (General Cox) argues that
there was no obstruction but Stuart's cavalry between Porter and Jackson, and an author of a defence of Porter (General George H. Gordon) calls
his report a romance. Stuart says that General Lee
arrived at Gainesville on the morning of the 29th
with Longstreet's corps ; that he passed his cavalry
through Longstreet's column and placed it on his
flank ; that during the day his videttes reported the
approach of Porter's corps ; and that he sent notice
of it to General Lee, who ordered infantry and
artillery to his support. He adds that in the mean

---

[1] Porter's corps camped at Bristoe the night of the 28th. About
6 o'clock on the morning of the 29th he was ordered by Pope
to Centreville. When he got near Bull Run he was ordered to
countermarch to Gainesville.

time he kept his cavalry dragging brush to raise a
dust, and that the ruse had the desired effect of
deceiving Porter. As Stuart was recovering Longstreet's flank he would be close to it. Now the object he had in dragging the brush was to deceive
Porter as to the force with which he was in immediate contact. His saying that Porter was deceived
by it was the mere expression of his opinion—not
the statement of a fact. Stuart's object was to gain
time enough for Longstreet (not Jackson) to read-
just his line to meet a threatened attack on his
flank. That was all. If Porter saw a heavy cloud
of dust rising in the road before him, he could not
tell, without halting his column and reconnoitring,
what created it. But the delay involved in doing
this was all that Stuart wanted. Longstreet had
been in the same dilemma at Salem two days
before ; when he reached there he met Buford's
cavalry. If he had known that nothing else was in
front of him, he would have brushed them away
with a few skirmishers without losing a minute on
his march. But he halted his column, he says, and
was detained an hour before he could find out what
it was. Pope was deceived by a few shells the Confederates threw at him across the Rappahannock
into the belief that our army was in his front when
in fact it was in his rear. The divine genius has
never yet appeared in war that could always at a

glance detect every stratagem and see through every mask. " He who wars," says Napier, " walks in a mist through which the keenest eye cannot always discern the right path."

The Military Society of Massachusetts has published a volume of papers on the Fitz John Porter case, which contains a letter from Gen. B. H. Robertson to Gen. Porter, in which he says, " There was no cavalry in that direction [Manassas Junction] *but mine*, which was held there the remainder of the day ;" and again he says : " I have no knowledge of bushes having been dragged by cavalry to create the impression of large forces coming, or for any purpose. Had these directions been given, the order would naturally have been transmitted through me. I heard no order on that subject." And Gen. Porter says, " There was no dragging of brush, nor such a project thought of, although Gen. Stuart so states in his report. Gen. Pope harps on it." The conclusion suggested is that the statement contained in Stuart's report is false, because *Robertson had never heard of it.*

" There are more things in heaven and earth than were ever dreamt of in your philosophy, Horatio !" Now, Gen. Robertson is mistaken in saying that we had no cavalry in the direction from which Porter approached *but his ;* Stuart was there in person with a part of Fitz Lee's brigade. Gen. Rosser, who was then a colonel in Lee's brigade, says : " When Stuart joined me he notified me that the enemy was moving on our right flank, and ordered me to move my command up and down the dusty road, and to drag brush, and thus create a heavy dust, as though troops were in motion. I kept this up at least four or five hours." Robertson was relieved by Stuart of his command immediately after the battle, and sent back to a camp of instruction. As Gen. Porter was not inside the Confederate lines that day, it is hard to understand how he could know that the brush was not dragged to raise a dust to deceive him, or that nothing of the sort was thought of. I am glad that he has been relieved of an unjust sentence ; but I am not willing to be silent now, when " young Harry Percy's spur is cold," and see his reputation sacrificed to save Gen. Porter's.